THE DAY I LOST

A FOUNDER'S JOURNEY THROUGH EVENTS AND LIFE

ROQUE QUADROS

ISBN 979-8-89066-865-3

"All life demands struggle. Those who have everything given to them become lazy, selfish and insensitive to the real values of life. The very striving and hard work that we so constantly try to avoid is the major building block in the person we are today."

– Pope Paul VI

ACKNOWLEDGEMENTS

I dedicate this book to all those who dare to dream. May you find the courage to turn those dreams into reality. You can achieve greatness if you believe in yourself and let your light shine brightly.

To those who have supported me through every step of this journey, thank you for your love and encouragement. Your belief in me has fuelled my determination.

To my teachers, thank you for sharing your wisdom and knowledge. Your impact on my life is beyond measure.

To my family, you are my rock and my guiding force. Your constant support and understanding have laid the foundation for my dreams to flourish. I want to express a special thank you to my sweet daughter Rheanne, whose relentless push to write this book has been instrumental in its creation. To my lovely wife Connie, your initiation and encouragement to pursue my passions, from events to writing, has been transformative. Without your support, I would not have achieved my dreams. And to my darling daughter Rochelle, whose contributions as both editor and cover designer have been invaluable. Your unwavering support has been a source of strength and comfort. Thank you for always being there when I needed you.

To all the readers, thank you for joining me on this adventure. I hope these words ignite a spark within you and empower you to chase after your dreams.

SPECIAL THANKS

TO MY ANGEL INVESTOR, MR MOHAMMED SAAD

I would like to express my deepest gratitude to an extraordinary person who has made a significant impact on my life. Mr Mohammed Saad is more than just my mentor or investor; he has shown immense care for my well-being and personal development. His unwavering support transformed me remarkably.

What sets Mr Mohammed apart is his selflessness and belief in my abilities. Despite being my employer and providing me with a salary, he went above and beyond by allowing me to pursue my business. His impact on my life extends beyond professional guidance. He has been a source of inspiration and support, nurturing my growth and helping me achieve my goals. I am forever grateful for the trust he placed in me, and I made it a point to honor and preserve that trust throughout my journey.

ABOUT MR MOHAMMED SAAD AL SHARIF

Mr Mohammed Saad Al Sharif is a distinguished public servant in Dubai. His journey as a member of the esteemed Dubai Police began with a deep sense of duty and a desire to make a meaningful difference in the vibrant and ever-evolving city.

Throughout his remarkable 35-year tenure with the Dubai Police, he used specialized knowledge to build a capable workforce and shape Dubai's law enforcement future.

Mr. Mohammed Saad Al Sharif earned recognition for his dedication and contributions during his service with the Dubai Police. A moment of immense pride came when His Highness Sheikh Mohammed bin Rashid Al-Makhtoum Vice President and Prime Minister of the United Arab Emirates and Ruler of Dubai himself gave upon him the highest honor - the recognition of their application as the best police application in the entire region. This recognition highlighted the team's impressive use of technology, making an impact on law enforcement.

As his career reached its culmination, Mr. Mohammed Saad Al Sharif found himself drawn to explore new avenues beyond his uniform. Retirement opened up diverse business possibilities, including in real estate and electromechanical sectors, while still dedicating himself to the community.

His dedication, compassion, and commitment have left a positive impact on the lives of countless individuals, contributing significantly to the growth and prosperity of Dubai.

CONTENTS

PREFACE

EVERYTHING STARTS WITH A DREAM

Welcome to my life in the event industry, a field that has been my passion for over two decades. Although this book is about the challenges faced over the years of working in events, it is not just a book about event management. I firmly believe that the lessons I learnt can be relevant to any business or daily life situations.

This is the story of how I started my business in the entertainment and event management industry, even though I had zero experience. Through imagination, dreams and taking action, I turned my ideas into reality. Along the way, I experienced moments of pressure, stress, fun, excitement, anger, and happiness. In retrospect, I realized the valuable lessons that shaped me into the person I am today.

This book provides you, the reader, with the strategies and insights that have guided me towards success in this dynamic industry. I aim to save you time and effort by sharing my experiences, both the struggles and triumphs, as a well of knowledge from which you can draw. This is especially valuable if you aspire to enter the world of event management.

I describe this industry as "Good from far, far from good" to show how demanding it is to produce events on time and with quality. While we heavily rely on our teams and freelancers, we can achieve anything by working in a focused and strategic manner.

I have had the privilege of working on various events, from conferences to product launches, awards night to fashion shows and musical concerts collaborating with clients from various backgrounds and industries.

However, event management is not without its challenges. The long hours, tight deadlines and unexpected surprises can create a high-stress environment. Therefore, it is crucial to build a sound foundation of skills, knowledge, and the right mindset to navigate these challenges and thrive in this field.

In the midst of learning about my experiences, there are also tips and tricks you can learn from to manage events effectively. I hope this book will inspire you to enhance your skills, no matter your experience level.

Thank you for joining me on this incredible journey. May this book serve as a source of inspiration and guidance as you pursue your dreams and create remarkable experiences for those around you. From this book, there are two key lessons to grasp: the importance of time management and the power of your dreams. Once you prioritize them, everything else will fall into place.

WHY I FLUNG
MY HIGH-PAYING JOB?

"The ultimate tragedy is not the oppression and cruelty by the bad people but the silence over that by the good people."

– Martin Luther King, Jr.

When I first started earning money, my primary goal was to focus on building a better life and making enough money to support myself. My initial salary in 1981 while I was working as an Air Condition mechanic was just Rs 50 a month, which is less than 1 US dollar today. It doesn't sound like much, but everyone has to start somewhere, right? During that time, life was really challenging, and there weren't many job opportunities available. We didn't have as many choices as we do today. However, I realised that I had to begin somewhere, even if it wasn't a high-paying job. It was the starting point of my journey towards financial stability and creating a comfortable life for myself.

While the job provided very little money, I enjoyed the family-like atmosphere. Positive people and a warm environment surrounded me from the start and I preferred that to a large salary and dealing with negativity. The job was no cakewalk considering the pressure, but I had my own working style planned out right from the start. I wanted to be in a place where I could learn, earn, and grow alongside the company. That was my mantra, and I stuck to it.

After working and waiting patiently for two long years, I finally got a call from an international oil drilling company inviting me for an interview. I prayed fervently because I knew deep down that this was the opportunity I had been waiting for to make my dreams a reality. I went for the interview- it lasted only 10 minutes. Then, the HR manager asked me to sit in his car. As soon as I sat in the car, he told me to wear my seatbelt and that was the first time I used my seatbelt and till date have continued doing so. I did not know where he was taking me. We drove to a massive workshop, and he told me to get started right away. I couldn't believe it!

They offered me a monthly stipend of Rs. 800 for the first three months, and once I completed the training, I would have a work schedule of 15 days on and 15 days off. The best part? My salary would increase to around Rs. 5000. The thought of my salary having two additional zeros in only three months was an incredible feeling. The rise was a complete 100%. The feeling that my dreams were being fulfilled had already begun.

I couldn't wait to get started when I joined the workplace. They asked me to change into a boiler suit and get to work. However, as soon as I began, I noticed my colleagues staring at me. One of them approached me and asked, "Who are you? Who helped you get this job?" At that moment, I didn't fully understand the significance of the job. All I knew is that in just three months, my salary would increase by a hundredfold.

Unfortunately, things took a turn for the worse right away. On my very first day, my supervisor started harassing me and assigned tasks that made me feel unwanted. Despite this, I was patient and did my best to adapt to working with someone like him. As the day was ending, it was time to change out of the boiler suit and back into my regular clothes. But when I did so along with my colleagues, I was unexpectedly questioned, "Who told you to change? The question shocked me, but the instructions were to put the boiler suit back on and return to work. He made me clean the oil-covered floor left by other team members. I did as I was told and after some time, I could finally leave. My first day at my new job left quite an impression on me.

As I went into work the second day, I was still hopeful. I changed into my boiler suit, but my supervisor asked me to observe without starting work. It seemed like my supervisor was testing my patience, maybe trying to harass me, or even afraid of having a new person around. It felt like he wanted to get rid of me as quickly as possible. When it was time for lunch, he approached me and told me to keep working. I reached my breaking point because they made me feel unwelcome and did not treat me as part of the team. It struck my mind that if I carry on like this, my life would be miserable. I always believed that at work, the most important thing was respect. I had reached my limit and decided that this high-paying job was not suitable for me. I walked up to him, expressed my gratitude for the opportunity, and left the place for good.

Feeling dejected, I decided to go back to the job where I was earning a meager Rs 50 per month. Despite the significantly lower pay, the atmosphere there felt like a close-knit family. It was a place where I felt more at ease and appreciated for who I was. My boss happily accepted me without a second thought.

At this oil rig operator's job, there was one thing I had always longed for: the chance to ride in a helicopter. It had been a dream of mine for a long time and for that sole reason; I took a chance working at this place. However, it always seemed like an unattainable goal. As a child, I never even could sit in a private car, so the idea of being in a helicopter felt like an unimaginable luxury. But now, with just three months in, the possibility of actually experiencing it felt truly amazing. I could hardly believe that something I had only dreamed of before was within reach.

But you know what? I strongly believe in destiny. I always say that life has its own plans for you. It will take you where you need to go, not necessarily where you want to go. So, I held onto that belief. I knew that if it happened, it would happen at the right time. I kept my hopes up and trusted that life had something amazing in store for me, even if it wasn't exactly what I had imagined.

Leaving my high-paying job after just two days took a lot of self-awareness and courage. It was difficult to walk away from something that seemed like a dream come true, especially when it meant giving up financial security.

I always knew what I wanted in my career - a place where I could learn, earn, and grow while being surrounded by positive people and a friendly atmosphere. The importance of having a supportive work environment was always higher on my list than a big salary. I understood the value of being part of a workplace family.

However, things changed when I joined the international company. I faced harassment from the supervisor, who seemed determined to get rid of me. This made me feel unwanted and unsupported. Despite the appeal of a high salary, I realized that the toxic work environment wasn't worth sacrificing my mental and emotional well-being.

It's crucial to understand that not all high-paying jobs are the same. While a big paycheck may be tempting, it's important to ponder the pros and cons of a job opportunity. Factors like work culture, management style, work-life balance, and job security all play a role in determining if a job is a good fit for you.

I quickly recognized when the job was a wrong fit. I decided to leave that job and return to a place where I felt a sense of belonging. Money no longer held the top priority. It was a risk, but it confirmed that I genuinely cared about my happiness and will take chances in order to discover a job that truly fulfilled me. Balancing financial stability and personal happiness should be our priority.

This international company is one of the top players in their field today. While I can wonder where life would have taken me had I stayed at the job, I have no regrets as it would not have given me the personal satisfaction and growth I reached today.

Choosing a career that makes us happy requires taking risks and exploring new opportunities. It may involve facing uncertainty and embracing the unknown. However, it is through this journey that we discover a job that aligns with our passions and values.

Pay attention to your inner voice and prioritize your well-being. Don't let the pursuit of money hinder you from living a deeply fulfilling life. It's time to take charge, forge your own path, and cultivate a career that truly lights up your soul.

MY MAIDEN TRIP

FOR BETTER PROSPECTS ABROAD

"I choose to make the rest of my life the best of my life."

– Louise Hay

AS A TRAVEL AGENT IN BOMBAY (MUMBAI)

When I began my journey in the travel industry in 1984, I felt incredibly excited. I had big dreams and a strong desire to explore fresh places and learn more about the world around me. In the beginning, my travel career was all about learning and growing. I sought opportunities to learn about different destinations and provide excellent customer service.

As a travel agent based in Bombay (now known as Mumbai), my primary focus was assisting individuals seeking job opportunities in Dubai. I handled passports and managed immigration procedures.

One of my primary duties was to ensure that all the documents and paperwork were in order, guaranteeing a hassle-free journey for the job seekers. I took special care of those who came from outside the city, working efficiently to arrange their travel accommodations promptly. This was crucial to minimize their expenses on daily accommodation. I enjoyed assisting people on their journey to a better life and making sure their experience was positive from Bombay to Dubai.

In my role as a travel agent, I took great care in verifying passports and ensuring travelers met all the requirements. Attention to detail was crucial, as even slight mistakes could cause delays. I stayed updated on regulations to provide accurate information and guidance. I understood the importance of my role in helping them start a new chapter in their lives.

After years of facilitating job opportunities for others in Dubai, I couldn't help but wonder what it would be like to experience the city myself. The stories I heard from people who had travelled there intrigued me. The more I heard, the more my curiosity grew, and I couldn't shake the feeling that I needed to see it for myself.

I had seen countless individuals embark on their journeys to the United Arab Emirates, chasing their dreams and seeking new prospects. The success stories and the vibrant energy surrounding the city made me realize that there was something special about Dubai.

The thriving economy and the city's reputation as a global business hub intrigued me. I wanted to be a part of it, to immerse myself in its unique mix of modernity and tradition and to see how I could grow both personally and professionally in such a dynamic environment. It was time for me to step out from behind the scenes and embark on my journey to Dubai, to see what it offered and to create my own unforgettable memories.

MY MAIDEN TRIP TO DUBAI

As I got on the plane, I felt a mix of excitement, nervousness, and a little sadness. My heavy suitcase seemed like a symbol of all these feelings. It reminded me of the memories and people I was leaving behind in Bombay. Looking out of the window as the plane took off, I said goodbye to the city lights and felt a wave of nostalgia.

Leaving my friends behind, who were always there for me, made me feel like a part of me was missing. I knew I would miss our spontaneous chai sessions and exploring the busy markets of Bombay together.

My family, who had always loved and supported me, now felt so far away. I thought about their smiles, warm hugs, and guidance, and it made me realize how much I would miss them in my everyday life.

But despite these emotions, there was also a spark of excitement. Dubai represented a fresh start, new opportunities, and a different way of life. The city was vibrant and full of diverse cultures and amazing architecture. I couldn't wait to immerse myself in this new world, make my path, and meet new people.

As the plane flew higher, I thought about the amazing journey ahead. It wasn't just a flight to a new country, but also a journey towards independence, personal growth, and discovering more about myself. The unknown future held so much potential. Leaving behind my friends, family, and the bustling lifestyle of Bombay was tough, but I knew it was the right decision.

Dubai seemed like the ideal place, with job prospects and the chance to have a successful career. Flying for the first time was a unique experience. I had witnessed many people in my life take flights, but this was my turn to fly through the skies.

Back in the late 80s, flights from India to the Middle East were not as abundant as they are today. We didn't have the luxury of countless options like we do now. It was a time when flights were not as affordable as they are today, so I felt a sense of privilege to get on this journey.

As the plane took off, I looked out the window and stared at the sight of the city below becoming smaller and smaller. It was an odd feeling, knowing that I was leaving everything familiar behind and venturing into the unknown. Little did I know that this first flight to Dubai would mark the beginning of a new chapter in my life.

WHEN I ARRIVED

As soon as I arrived in Dubai, my priority was to start my job hunt. The primary method for job searching was through daily newspapers. Online job opportunities weren't around back then.

To secure a job, you either needed a referral from someone you knew or you had to respond to contact numbers advertised in newspapers. The most successful approach was to print out multiple copies of your CV and visit companies to submit your resume. If an interviewer wasn't interested in offering you a job, they would often inquire about whether you had a driving license. They knew that gaining a driving license within a short period was quite challenging. Getting a driving license was like earning a badge of honor, granting you the ability to live and work in Dubai.

Throughout my school days, I never shared chocolates or celebrated my birthday by giving out sweets, while everyone else did. When I got my driving license, that too on my first try, which was no simple task, it felt like an enormous accomplishment. To celebrate this special moment, I shared sweets with my colleagues on the bus. It was the first time I ever shared treats, and it was a memorable experience for me.

EARLY DAYS IN DUBAI

During my early days, I encountered many challenges, especially for finding a job. Employers usually wanted candidates with regional experience. It was a difficult situation, but I never gave up.

Sending out thousands of CVs showed the commitment to exploring various opportunities and casting a wide net. Attending hundreds of interviews showcased the willingness to learn from each experience and refine one's interview skills. Persevering through rejections showed resilience and determination.

The U.A.E. offered an exceptional living experience, but it's vital to acknowledge and follow the local customs and regulations. The country offers limitless opportunities for exploration and the realization of your dreams. We know the Emirati people for their warm hospitality and friendly nature. They embrace individuals from all walks of life, making you feel at home in their country.

DUBAI IN THE 80S AND EARLY 90S

Dubai in the 80s and early 90s was a whole different world compared to what it is today. It's hard to believe that the Dubai we know now would be unrecognizable to those who experienced it during those days. I recall the days of driving from Dubai to Abu Dhabi on Sheikh Zayed Road, with only two lanes, no high rise buildings around, and occasional tea stops.

There are so many memories that come flooding back from that era, and anyone who was in Dubai and the UAE during the 1990s would surely have their own fond recollections. Places like the Karama shopping complex, Sana Fashion, Al Nasr Cinema, and Al Nasr Leisureland hold a special place in our hearts. The Dubai news channel, known as Channel 33, was a significant source of infotainment during that time.

One of the most memorable road trip destinations during that period was Hili Fun City in Al Ain. It was an experience to remember, and many people would plan trips there to enjoy the rides and attractions. Another notable change was witnessing the transformation of the Chicago Beach Hotel into what is now known as the Jumeirah Beach Hotel. I vividly remember driving along Jumeirah Road and witnessing the hotel being demolished as I was on my way to a meeting. It was a fantastic sight and a reminder of how quickly Dubai was evolving.

Thinking back on those years brings a sign of remembrance. Dubai and the UAE have undergone tremendous development and growth since then. It's remarkable to see how a once-deserted strip has transformed into a vibrant city. The memories of Dubai in the 80s and early 90s serve as a reminder of the rich history and remarkable journey that the city has taken.

DUBAI WAS A BLESSING

I felt truly blessed to be in Dubai and witness its incredible growth. I still remember when I read about the Dubai World Trade Centre being the tallest building in the U.A.E. at 38 stories in my daughter's history book. But now, we have the astonishing Burj Khalifa, the tallest man-made structure in the world. It's a testament to the remarkable progress and development Dubai has achieved.

Dubai has earned its reputation as the "shopping capital of the Middle East." With around 70 shopping centres, including the magnificent The Dubai Mall, one of the largest in the world, it's a shopaholic's paradise.

We adorn the city with breathtaking skyscrapers, state-of-the-art buildings, and captivating sand dunes. It's no wonder that millions of people visit Dubai each year to experience all that it offers. Dubai has something for everyone with its vibrant markets, cosy cafes, luxurious hotels and resorts.

When I think back to my early days in Dubai, iconic landmarks flood my mind. The Dubai Clock Tower, Flame roundabout, sailing dhows (abras), Al Maktoum Bridge and Dubai World Trade Centre are all ingrained in my mind. They were a part of the city's landscape and hold a special place in my heart. Introducing the metro system in 2009 reduced the value of driving licenses among people in Dubai. When I first arrived in the late 80s, buses and taxis were the major modes of transportation. The city has since evolved tremendously, especially in terms of transportation infrastructure, with the metro playing a key role in providing efficient and convenient travel options for everyone.

MY PATH

THROUGH VARIOUS JOBS TO MAKE MY DREAMS A REALITY

"Opportunities don't happen, you create them."

– Chris Grosser.

Destiny and correct timing often go hand in hand and can be labelled as moments of pure luck. Throughout our lives, we encounter situations where certain events align perfectly, leading us to opportunities or experiences that have a significant impact on our journey.

On my journey from Bombay to Dubai in 1989, I believe that destiny played a role in guiding me to the right path. When I first arrived in Dubai, I faced many challenges in finding suitable employment. It seemed like I was constantly hitting dead ends and facing rejections, which made me question whether I had made the right decision to move to a new country.

However, just when I was on the verge of losing hope, an unexpected opportunity presented itself. I came across a job opening in the travel sector that perfectly matched my skills and aspirations. It felt like the universe was leading me towards this opportunity. It was as if I was at the right place at the right time, and everything fell into place.

While it initially seemed like I stumbled upon this job because of pure luck, it was actually a combination of good timing and my perseverance through the obstacles I faced leading up to this moment. This experience taught me the importance of having faith in the journey and believing that things will work out when the time is right.

Throughout life, there are countless examples of people finding success or meeting influential individuals just by being at the right place at the right time. Random encounters can change our lives - finding a business partner, meeting a mentor, or landing a dream job.

It's crucial to keep in mind that success isn't entirely based on luck and destiny. Staying persistent, adaptable, and trusting our instincts is key to making the most of the opportunities. So, while we may experience moments of pure luck, it is ultimately our attitude and actions that shape our path and lead us towards fulfilling experiences and meaningful accomplishments.

After going through several job changes and feeling unsatisfied, I eventually landed this job that brought a sense of hope and excitement into my life. Little did I know that this would also connect me with my future angel investor. This moment was a turning point that marked the start of my extraordinary journey as an entrepreneur.

As I settled into my new job, I began noticing a series of coincidences and small signs that seemed to align perfectly. These coincidences eventually led me to a moment where it felt like the universe was guiding me in the right direction. This experience filled me with a sense of purpose and reaffirmed my belief that I was on the right path towards a remarkable journey.

When I reflect on the past, I feel comforted because the highs and lows, career shifts, and tough times all brought me to this. It was as if every step of my journey had been preparing me for this moment, and the stars had aligned to set my entrepreneurial dreams in motion.

BUILDING DREAMS

STORY BEHIND MY COMPANY'S FORMATION

"No one changes the world who isn't obsessed."

– Billie Jean King

During 1997, I worked in a Dubai travel office where my role involved managing the office and ensuring travelers had seamless travel experiences. I found my job to be satisfying and had formed a special attachment to it. However, everything changed when I received two exciting job offers from different airlines in Dubai. Both offers arrived simultaneously, providing me with a thrilling yet difficult decision to make.

On one hand, the job offers from the airlines promised better wages and increased job security. It was a tempting prospect that I couldn't ignore. My current job held a special place in my heart. I had a supportive boss, a familiar work environment, and a fantastic team. We had a great relationship, and I genuinely enjoyed the working atmosphere.

The decision to choose one option over the other was not just about financial benefits. It involved considering the long-term implications of my overall happiness and job satisfaction. I faced a crucial decision point in my life where I had to evaluate the consequences and pick the path that aligned with my ambitions.

I was constantly driven to take my skills and knowledge to new heights. I longed to explore new chances and take on new challenges. I was uncertain about how to start or take the leap.

Every day, after work, I would follow a routine with my Emirati boss. We would walk together towards his car, engaging in casual conversations. During these talks, I would talk about how I spent the day cultivating creativity and positivity in the office. However, the question about the job offers from the airlines was always in the back of my mind, lingering and demanding my attention.

Informing my boss about my decision was daunting. I was afraid of leaving the familiar and stepping into the unknown.

The thought of working under someone else made me wonder if I would find the same enjoyable work environment elsewhere. These doubts troubled me, and I also felt a sense of guilt for considering other career prospects.

One evening, I finally found the courage to have an open conversation with my boss. I explained my decision to resign from the company and explore alternative career paths after receiving job offers from airlines. I wasn't afraid of facing my boss; it was a matter of respect and not wanting to do something that felt wrong. Nevertheless, I felt it was crucial to inform him promptly to avoid any future regrets.

To my surprise, when my boss heard about my decision, he didn't convince me otherwise. Instead, he posed a question that caught me off guard: "What would make you happy to continue working with us?" It was an unexpected response that made me pause and reflect.

Considering the financial responsibilities of the company, I didn't want to burden him by asking for a salary increase. I couldn't imagine entering a business transaction with my boss, who was like family to me. So, in that moment, I turned to fate for guidance, and something unexpected happened.

"I want to start an entertainment company." Came out of my mouth spontaneously, with no prior planning. Entertainment businesses were less common and established in the UAE back then.

My boss listened to me carefully, and then simply said "Okay!". I was obviously stunned, realizing he had given me the green light to pursue my ambitious idea.

In the days that followed, I began contemplating how to turn my dream into a reality. A simple "okay" ignited a spark within me, a determination to prove that I could make this venture successful. Looking back now, I realize that his simple response was more than just an agreement. It was a show of trust and support, a belief in my potential that I hadn't fully recognized myself.

To set up the company, he asked me to come up with five name options, which was the first step in the company formation process. I provided the list of names as per the department's guidelines for obtaining my license. Surprisingly, the name I had a strong preference for was selected. On November 19, 1997, my company '4 Seasons Entertainment' came into existence.

Within a few days, I received my license. My boss handed it to me while I was still working in his office. I continued to work for him until I could get my company off the ground. However, I never conducted any personal business during office hours.

During the late '90s, entertainment and event management were not common or well-known in the UAE. However, I saw the UAE as a land of opportunity and came to Dubai to explore and make the most of any chances that came my way. I wanted to tap into the potential of the entertainment industry and create something unique and valuable.

The journey wasn't without its challenges, but with the support and trust of my boss, I took the leap to pursue my dream of starting an entertainment company. His belief in me gave me the confidence to venture into the unknown.

Launching a business with no initial capital was definitely challenging, but my experience has taught me it's possible. Turning business dreams into a successful venture is possible with the help of determination and mentorship, even in the face of financial limitations.

Now, I want to share the story of how that "okay" changed my life and set me on a path toward entrepreneurship. It taught me the value of seizing unexpected opportunities and believing in myself, even when the road ahead seemed uncertain. This turning point shaped my journey in event management and my life.

BELIEVE YOU CAN!

MY JOURNEY AS A BUSINESS OWNER

"Some people want it to happen, some wish it would happen, others make it happen."

– Michael Jordan

Even though I knew very little about entertainment businesses, I had a strong feeling that this industry had a scope that I could thrive in. My dream was to support and promote talented musicians and entertainers. I was nervous and unsure when I received my license. The entertainment industry was new to me, and my travel background made me doubt myself. But, because I grew up in a musical family, I had a deep desire to help musicians and bands succeed. This passion drove me to create a platform to help talented artists flourish.

To overcome my lack of knowledge, I took it upon myself to learn everything I could about the entertainment industry. I set clear goals and focused on understanding the financial aspects of running a business in this field. It was like solving a puzzle, piecing together unique elements until I had a simple plan in front of me.

But having a plan wasn't enough. I needed connections and support to make my dream a reality. So, I tried to get in touch with musicians and bands. I attended shows in search of artists who shared my vision. With every interaction, my brand took shape. I created a name, logo, and a visual identity that would capture people's hearts and minds.

I searched for hidden gems among talented musicians and bands. I sought them out in small venues where their music filled the air with emotion. Even though I was a newcomer to this vast entertainment world, I was ready to learn, grow, and adapt along the way. I knew challenges would arise, but I was ready to face them head-on.

I was determined to make a difference, to uplift and promote the artists whose melodies would touch people's hearts for years to come. Deep in my heart, I knew this journey would be worth every step.

Beginning a business can seem like an enormous task, especially when you're not sure where to start. But I figured out that it all begins with knowing what I'm passionate about and what I'm good at. So, I sat at my table with a blank piece of paper and a pen, ready to dive into some self-reflection. I thought about the things that truly made me excited and the skills that I possessed. What am I great at? What activities bring me joy and fulfilment? These thoughts and ideas became my guide, pointing me in the right direction as I explored distinct possibilities. They gave me the confidence and determination to start my business.

I knew I had to do some research. Back then, I had to go hunting for every opportunity that came my way, big or small. The methods of reaching out to clients were completely different compared to today. Fax machines and phone calls were the primary means of communication, unlike the surplus of options we have now. Besides, the primary sources of information were newspapers and TV, along with the trusty telephone directory and yellow pages. Since I came from the travel industry, this industry was a whole new world for me. To my best knowledge, there were no existing companies to study and learn from.

Today, there are many ways to connect with clients, and the most effective method depends on your business, target audience, and marketing goals. You can use email, newsletters, and social media such as Facebook, Instagram, Twitter and LinkedIn. These platforms allow you to share updates, build relationships, and promote your business. Your website is crucial, as it often serves as the first point of contact for potential clients. It's important to ensure that it is well-designed and optimised for search engines.

When I compare the ways of reaching clients when I first started my business to today, the difference is amazing. The current methods are not only more effective but also much easier to target the right clients for your products and services. It's incredible how technology has revolutionised the way we do business.

My aim was to identify the gaps in the entertainment business through market research and determine how I could bridge them. I rigorously searched through newspapers, dissecting trends and capturing people's interests. To understand what appeals to viewers, I turned on the television and watched a range of shows and programs. A search was conducted by me for contacts in the directory and yellow pages. I started calls, contacted individuals, and began collecting information.

It was a time-consuming process, but it was necessary. I had to familiarize myself with this fresh territory and figure out how I could provide something unique and valuable. I studied the market, identified the gaps, and began brainstorming ideas on how to bridge them.

Not having any established entertainment companies to learn from was a challenge, so I used it as a chance to create my path and bring new ideas. I was determined to create a business that would stand out and meet the needs of people uniquely.

Research illuminated my understanding of the market and customer preferences. With this knowledge, I could create an entertainment company that met the audience's demands and desires.

While it limited the resources compared to today's digital age, I made the most of what was available. It was a journey of discovery, learning, and adaptation. And with each piece of information I gathered, I became more equipped to enter the entertainment industry and make a meaningful impact.

After spending a few days scribbling on paper, I realized it was time to prioritize and tackle the most important task at hand. I needed to create a business plan—a blueprint that would help me organize my ideas, define my goals, and outline a strategy to achieve them. This plan included identifying my target market, developing strategies, making projections, and determining implementation.

During this process, I asked important questions. Where could I find individuals or organizations that would be interested in my services? Who should I connect with to kick start my business? What topics should I discuss with potential clients? Who were the people that truly needed the services I offered?

I knew that success wouldn't come without effort. I was prepared to invest my time and energy into building my business. Even though I lacked a role model in my specific field, I remained determined to carve my path and learn from the experiences along the way. There were no experienced individuals I could turn to for insights because I hadn't seen others go through a similar process before.

I realized that the first step to kick start my business was to define my brand identity clearly. This meant figuring out the personality, values, and mission of my company. It was important to understand what made my business unique and what it stood for. This knowledge would guide me in designing the perfect logo.

Choosing the right font and colours was crucial in reflecting my brand identity and attracting my target audience. I wanted my logo to make a powerful impact, so I used the colours red and black. These colours helped my logo stand out and grab people's attention.

To bring my logo ideas to life, I began sketching them out. By sketching, I could visualize and refine my design. It made it easier for me to see what elements worked well together and what needed improvement. Sketching helped me fine-tune the details and create a logo that truly represented my business.

Designing my logo was an exciting and creative process. It allowed me to showcase the personality and essence of my company visually. With the right font, colours, and sketches, I could craft a logo that captured the essence of my brand and made a memorable impression on my audience.

Creating a logo that would stand out and be memorable was crucial for my business. I understood the logo would represent everything I stood for, so it had to be unique. Along with the logo, I needed a catchy tagline that would explain what I do and how I do it. That's when I came up with the name and the tagline "Think of an event...We make it happen!"

The logo and tagline were completed, announcing a new company's arrival. I started by using the logo on my business cards and other printed materials. I printed brochures and flyers to spread the word about my services. It felt like an enormous accomplishment, but now I needed to figure out who my clients were and where to send these materials.

After creating my logo and tagline, the next step was identifying my target clients and finding the right channels to share my materials. At first, I encountered difficulties when attempting to contact potential clients directly..

To overcome this challenge, I came up with a strategic approach: I decided to approach hotels and offer my entertainment services to them. This strategy made sense because hotels often require entertainment options for their guests. By collaborating with hotels, I could address their needs while also creating a strong foundation of clients for my business.

This approach turned out to be quite effective. Not only did it allow me to establish a reliable client base, but it also provided me with valuable hands-on experience within the entertainment industry. Working closely with hotels taught me the ropes of the business and gave me insights into what customers in the hospitality sector truly value.

In essence, my decision to collaborate with hotels was a well-thought-out move. It helped me overcome the initial challenges of reaching out directly and paved the way for both professional growth and success in the entertainment industry.

BOOKING MY FIRST BAND

A MEMORABLE STEP INTO THE ENTERTAINMENT WORLD

"Inspiration does exist, but it must find you working."

– Pablo Picasso

As I began meeting with hotels to discuss their entertainment needs, my thoughts turned to my hometown, Goa, India. Goa is famous for its lively musical tradition and the people of Goa have a deep love and appreciation for music. It is a part of their daily life, from social events to religious ceremonies.

GOA: AN ENCHANTING PARADISE OF MELODIES

Goa is a state on the southwestern coast of India. It is renowned for its beaches, nightlife, architecture and culture. As a Goan, one can experience a laid-back and relaxed lifestyle. The people of Goa, known as Goans, are known for their warm hospitality and friendly nature. They take pride in their local traditions, music, and dance forms such as the famous folk dance, Fugdi, and the traditional Konkani music.

I realised that the musical richness of Goa is something that was worth focusing on through my entertainment company. The local musicians and bands in Goa possessed a unique style that could fascinate listeners. I could showcase the incredible musical culture of my hometown by bringing Goan musicians and bands into the entertainment scene. It was a chance to celebrate the tradition and talent of Goa while providing top-notch entertainment services to the hotels and their guests.

Visiting Goa became a priority for me. I wanted to connect with talented musicians, bands, artists and build partnerships. I found inspiration and created meaningful ties with the Goan musicians on my journey back to my roots.

Goan music is full of life, with catchy beats, beautiful melodies, and a wide range of instruments. When you listen to Goan music, you can't help but tap your feet and feel the rhythm in your heart. The music of Goa is a fusion of different styles and influences. It's like a delicious mix of Indian, Portuguese, and Western flavours. Traditional Indian sounds combine with lively Portuguese and modern Western tunes.

Instruments like the Saxophone, mandolin, guitar, and violin are commonly used in Goan music. They add a unique touch to the compositions and create a rich and mixed sound. Each instrument has its own role to play, coming together to create a piece of music. I grew up listening to my father play the Alto Saxophone, Violin and Clarinet for hours.

So, with Goa as my destination, I hopped on a plane and set off on a journey to discover the musical heart of this amazing place. My plan was to bring a piece of Goa's appealing music to hotels and make sure everyone who experienced it had a mind-blowing time.

THE JOURNEY OF BOOKING BANDS

After deciding to bring the musical talents of Goa to hotels in Dubai, the next step was to take action. For selecting and meeting bands for these contracts, there were some important steps I followed. I researched bands with the correct style and musical talent that would be compatible with the hotel's atmosphere.

To ensure a successful partnership between the bands and the hotel, the first thing I had to do was to understand the hotel's needs and goals for the residency. I needed to know what kind of music they were looking for and who their target audience was. Understanding their goals was crucial in selecting the right bands.

To gather this information, I asked myself questions like: What type of music would best suit the hotel's ambiance and atmosphere? What kind of experience do they want to provide for their guests? These questions helped me understand the hotel's preferences and requirements.

Once I had a list of potential bands, I reached out to them and arranged meetings to get to know them better. I analysed their music, stage presence and professionalism during the meetings. It was important for me to ensure that the bands not only had the musical talent but also a professional and reliable approach.

I outlined the hotel residency contract for the bands, including schedule, payment, and expectations. It was crucial to establish clear communication and a mutual understanding of the terms and conditions. I considered the band's availability, travel to Dubai and the ability to meet requirements. Finding bands that could deliver exceptional performances was essential.

After considering all options, I chose the bands that best fit the hotel's needs. I ensured that all necessary paperwork and contracts were in place, providing a solid foundation for a successful partnership. Careful planning and evaluation were needed for sourcing and selecting bands.

Within a few days, I had narrowed down my options and created a shortlist of potential bands for the residency. The next step was to schedule meetings with these bands to delve deeper into the details of the collaboration. It was an exciting chance to chat with the band members and get details about their experience and availability.

To meet with over 19 bands, each having their own members, I needed to find a good place for these meetings. I wanted a friendly environment where we could understand each other's wants.

During these meetings, we focused on discussing the residency in greater detail. I wanted to ensure that the bands were not only talented, but also united with the vision and goals of the project. We discussed their experiences, musical style, and adaptability.

We ensured they could commit to the residency and performance requirements. Open and honest communication was key to establishing a sound foundation for our collaboration.

Everything was running smoothly and efficiently. We were all dedicated to the project and focused on achieving our shared goals. The meetings fostered connections and created an enthusiasm for the residency.

The process of meeting with potential bands was an important step in ensuring that we had the right partners for the project. We evaluated their qualifications and built a strong working relationship. With each meeting, we grew closer to assembling a remarkable lineup of bands that would bring the hotel's entertainment vision to life.

CHALLENGES THAT CROPPED UP

It was time to negotiate the terms of the contract with the chosen bands. Negotiations included settling the date, time, and compensation.

During this process, it was crucial for me to express my expectations and what I would offer clearly. I had to be open to compromise and find a mutually agreeable solution. The goal was to reach a fair agreement that would benefit both the bands and the hotel.

As an agency, one of my primary responsibilities was to ensure a solid understanding between the bands, the hotel, and myself. To formalise this understanding, I created a Memorandum of Understanding (MOU). This document outlines the terms and details of the agreement between all parties involved. It helps establish a broad understanding of the partnership, collaboration, or joint project. The MOU outlines the agreement, responsibilities, duration, and financial commitments. It serves as a written agreement that provides a foundation for further negotiations and collaboration.

A successful business deal requires three parties to understand each other and be satisfied with the outcome. These parties are the client, the supplier (or artists) and the agency. The client needs a service or product and plays a big role in the deal. The supplier or artists are the ones who provide the goods or services, and it's their job to give high-quality products that satisfy the client's needs. As the agency, I acted as the intermediary, managing the transaction between the client and the supplier.

The MOU was a crucial tool in this process. It outlined the terms and details of the partnership, ensuring that everyone was on the same page. It provided a legal framework that protected the bands and guaranteed a fair working relationship. However, some bands seemed hesitant in signing the MOU, despite my clarifications. They failed to grasp that the purpose of the MOU was to protect them legally and ensure a fair and beneficial partnership.

After days of hard work, meeting with various bands and facing the possibility of returning empty-handed, I was determined not to give up. Fortunately, luck was on my side. During my journey back to Dubai via Bombay (now Mumbai), I received a referral to a well-connected gentleman in Bombay who managed several bands.

I had a brief meeting with him, lasting only 30 minutes, but it turned out to be a stroke of luck. He understood my situation and introduced me to one of his bands. Within a day, we could sign an MOU, solidifying our partnership. With the signed performance contract in hand, I made my way back to Dubai.

When I got back, I worked on promoting the band to hotel clients. I visited several hotels and promoted the band, highlighting why they would be a perfect fit for their residency. In a short period, I received a positive response from an international hotel chain. They agreed to sign a contract with me for the band, and within a month, the band was flown to Dubai.

THE REMARKABLE HOTEL RESIDENCY: A TURNING POINT FOR MY ENTERTAINMENT BUSINESS

The entertainment contract was initially planned as a three month hotel residency exceeded all expectations. The remarkable success of the venture led to an extension of the contract, stretching beyond the initial timeframe. This turning point proved to be a significant milestone for my entertainment business, taking it to the next level of professionalism and receiving noteworthy acclaim from the industry.

It all started with my first band booking, and from there, I ventured into booking many bands and entertainers for various occasions. I successfully contracted with hotels, corporate events, product launches and shopping festivals. As my experience grew, so did my reputation.

Word got around about the experiences I provided, and soon, bands, entertainers, musicians, and singers were lining up to work with me.

"A Reliable Bridge between Artists and Clients" is a compelling tagline that perfectly captures the mission of the entertainment agency. Talented artists and clients are brought together by the agency. The tagline stresses mutual partnerships and satisfaction.

The journey to booking my first band taught me the invaluable lessons of perseverance and seizing opportunities. Despite the initial challenges I encountered, I remained determined and refused to give up. I broadened collaborations by networking with artists from different backgrounds. In just a few years, I achieved a significant milestone by connecting with over 2000 international, regional, and Bollywood artists.

Maintaining determination during tough times can ultimately yield to positive outcomes. Confronting difficulties with unwavering resolve and building connections can lead to remarkable achievements. In short, the chapter's message is to persist, network, and benefit from our efforts.

FROM SOLO TO PARTNERSHIP

WHY I NEEDED A PARTNER

"I can do things you cannot, you can do things I cannot; together we can do great things."

– Mother Teresa

As I booked more artists, I slowly started seeing an overall growth. A multitude of hotels and clients who wanted to hire entertainers and bands started reaching out. It was at this point that I realised that more and more people were recognising my business and the influence it was having in the industry. Running a business can be tough, and it's not always smooth sailing. You often encounter various problems that can be quite challenging to solve.

CHALLENGES FACED IN ENGAGING CLIENTS FOR FUTURE EVENTS

A difficulty I faced early in my business was when I would arrange for bands and entertainers to perform at my clients' events. For their first event, there wasn't a concern, as I would get paid for each event I organised. However, after the event, I saw clients stopped replying to my messages or calls and wouldn't book another event. This situation puzzled me, and I started asking myself several questions to understand why this was happening.

One reason could be that the clients were not satisfied with the performances of the bands and entertainers I had sent. The bands may not have met the clients' standards. If this was the case, it was understandable that they wouldn't want to hire my services again.

Another possibility is that there was a miscommunication or misunderstanding between me and the clients. Maybe they had certain expectations or requirements that were not properly conveyed to the bands and entertainers. As a result, the event might not have turned out as the clients had imagined, leading to dissatisfaction.

It's also essential to consider the possibility that the clients simply had a change in their event planning preferences. They may have found different ways to book entertainment. In such cases, it's not necessarily a suggestion of the quality of the bands and entertainers I provided, but a change in the clients' own preferences.

THE SIGNIFICANCE OF SELF-REFLECTION AS A BUSINESS OWNER AND EVENT ORGANIZER

It was important to reflect on my performance as a business owner and event organiser continuously. Was my communication with the clients effective throughout the process? Did I address any concerns or issues promptly? If I failed to meet their expectations in any of these areas, it could have contributed to their decision not to work with me again.

To find answers and improve my business, I would first need to find the root of the problem. I reached out to the clients, who stopped responding and ask for feedback. They could provide valuable information about what went wrong or what could be improved. I would review my communication and customer service to provide the best experience.

I might consider diversifying my pool of bands and entertainers to cater to a wider range of client preferences. Thorough auditions and background checks are needed to ensure I'm working with event-ready performers.

Evaluating customer satisfaction, communication, preferences and performance are essential for understanding business challenges. Addressing these areas was essential to keep clients. I asked myself the following questions to understand the situation better:

Did I communicate effectively with my clients?

Were there any misunderstandings between me and my clients?

Were my clients too busy to plan another event?

Did my client feel dissatisfied with my service?

I reflected on these questions to identify the cause of my clients' reluctance. Self-assessment revealed areas to improve, such as communication, customer satisfaction, and external factors. Equipped with these valuable insights, I could now take proactive steps to address any shortcomings and foster stronger and more successful business relationships in the future.

EXPLORING SUPPORT OPTIONS DURING BUSINESS CHALLENGES

Finding the right support during business difficulties can be hard. I needed someone to talk to, but it was difficult to find someone who truly understood my unique business. Even though friends and family could provide emotional support, they would not know enough about my industry to give helpful advice. Clients might not fully understand my business, so their suggestions may not solve my challenges.

Seeking guidance from other business owners might be tough if they're not familiar with my line of work. They may have expertise in different industries that didn't match my needs.

So I looked at alternative options. I checked out professional networks or communities where business owners face similar challenges. Hiring a business coach or consultant with expertise in my field could also be a good idea. They could give personalised guidance and strategies to tackle my challenges.

The more I thought about it, the more I realised how complex my problem was. Clients weren't responding, and I didn't want to question the band members directly. Since I wasn't at the events, I couldn't see how the bands performed or how the audience reacted.

Without direct feedback from clients, it was hard to figure out why they weren't responding or what needed improvement. Plus, it was challenging to check the bands' backgrounds or ensure consistent quality because they were freelancers.

CONSIDERING HIRING STAFF VS. FINDING A WORKING PARTNER

While positive responses were coming in, I knew they wouldn't last forever. In the absence of simple answers, my intuition became my reliable guide. In business, relying on intuition can be valuable, especially with incomplete information. It prompted me to think differently.

One question I asked myself was whether to hire staff or find a partner. I weighed the pros and cons:

Hiring Staff:

Pros: More control, ability to shape the staff, potential loyalty

Cons: Increased financial responsibility, management challenges, finding reliable employees

Working with a Partner:

Pros: Shared workload and responsibilities, access to expertise and resources

Cons: Shared decision-making, potential disagreements

Considering these factors, I aimed to determine the more suitable option for my business.

Among the pros and cons, the concept of shared decision-making and responsibility stood out. For example, in my artist agency, hiring staff would give me control, but all decision-making would be my responsibility. Working together would let us decide and share success.

I looked for a working partner to benefit from shared decision-making. Their involvement would bring fresh perspectives and collective responsibility for the business prosperity.

THE BENEFITS OF WORKING WITH A PARTNER IN BUSINESS

Shared responsibility: Having a partner means sharing responsibility for the business. This leads to increased commitment and dedication, as both partners have a personal stake in the company's success. Working partners can make quick decisions and take actions that benefit the business. This ability helps the company to respond effectively to market changes.

Willingness to go the extra mile: Working partners often show a higher level of dedication, as they have a direct stake in the business' success. They are motivated to work harder and go above and beyond to achieve positive outcomes.

Lower cost: Working with a partner can be a cost-effective option compared to hiring staff. Partners may accept a smaller salary or take a smaller share of profits for a greater stake in the business.

I looked for a partner with availability during unconventional hours, and the ability to drive results. I needed someone who could work late nights and contribute significantly to the growth and success of my business.

Finding the right partner takes time and effort, but it's worth it for the business.

THE POWER OF TRUSTING YOUR INTUITION IN DECISION-MAKING

When faced with challenges and a lack of support, I had to make quick decisions based on my intuition. Despite the uncertainty, I went ahead with having a working partner, trusting my gut feeling. This choice turned out to be a game-changer, leading to positive transformations in my business.

During my tenure at a travel agency affiliated with a group of companies, I encountered an individual who consistently showed a keen interest in collaborating with me. He exhibited a genuine liking for my company, and although we hadn't initially discussed business matters, there was a favourable rapport between us. While the idea of business wasn't at the forefront of my thoughts back then, circumstances eventually led me to consider this avenue.

Whilst contemplating the idea of having a working partner instead of hiring more staff, this gentleman was the first individual to come to my mind. His unwavering belief in me and his willingness to heed my directions left a powerful impression. He was a young professional willing to invest odd hours in his work, with the advantage of being a bachelor and having no qualms about staying late into the night. This aspect was pivotal in my decision-making process to not stay at events and spend late nights away from my family. This solidified him as a potential partner in my mind.

When it seems impossible to find help and there is little hope, listening to your intuition can be crucial. Intuition taps into our inner wisdom and guides us when logical answers are not readily available. It can provide valuable insights and point us in the right direction.

Trusting my intuition allowed me to make a bold decision that significantly impacted my business. It reminded me that sometimes we need to rely on our instincts and take risks, even in uncertain circumstances. Intuition can be a powerful tool when all other options seem limited or unclear.

When faced with challenges, letting my intuition guide me led to unexpected and positive outcomes. It is a reminder to listen to that inner voice and allow it to guide you when you need it the most.

LESSONS LEARNED

FROM MY EARLY YEARS AS A BUSINESS OWNER

"Don't let people fool you when in trouble"

– Roque Quadros

Within just a few years of starting my business, I found myself plunge into a thrilling adventure - organising a musical concert! The thing is, I had never been to a concert before and had no experience in event planning. But I thrive on challenges, so I eagerly dived in. Meticulous planning and an eye for detail were crucial for us to create the magical experience we envisioned.

Being a dreamer, I dived into this concert planning journey with enthusiasm, knowing it could be both complex and rewarding. I genuinely believed in my ability to deliver an unforgettable experience to everyone involved. Despite my enthusiasm, I had doubts - could I really gather a crowd of 500+?

When handling events on a larger scale, there is one significant hurdle: Financial support. I would need to obtain sponsors to make this dream come true.

I realised the key to success was understanding the difference between a wonderful event and a successful one. While both bring joy and delight to attendees, a successful event goes beyond that, delivering increased revenue.

With each passing day, the pressure that we felt mounted, and the deadline became increasingly tight, leaving us just 45 days to bring this grand vision to life. It was at that moment when I figured that getting the sponsorships we needed was beyond our capabilities and that we required the help of an expert.

With the help of some friends, we found a freelance sponsorship partner who was referred to as a pro in managing sponsorships. We put our trust in his expertise to ensure a smooth ride. Unfortunately, things didn't turn out as we had hoped. We could not make progress because of unproductive conversations, even after attending several meetings and discussions. Being a person of action, I have always valued time as a precious commodity.

Determined to take charge, I took things into my own hands. We somehow had to "Make things happen" as our company's tagline says so. Time was crucial and I couldn't depend entirely on someone else. I had to secure sponsorships and found a practical way to do so.

I stepped out of my comfort zone and reached out to potential sponsors. I reached out to whoever I could think of and then some - airlines, radio stations, newspapers and corporate clients. And the result paid off! Despite the difficulty of securing cash sponsors, I could secure a remarkable array of in-kind sponsors who believed in our vision.

As the clock relentlessly ticked away, we proceeded with the event. The lack of cash sponsors didn't deter us; we were determined to create an unforgettable experience for all attendees.

In the process of event organisation, there are two primary categories of sponsors: paid sponsors and in-kind sponsors

Paid sponsors are companies or individuals who provide financial support for the event. They give us cash in exchange for their branding to be visible at the event. This way, we get support to pay for rentals, marketing and talent while they get to market their company to the event attendees.

In-kind sponsors contribute valuable goods or services rather than monetary donations. They might offer free products, equipment, catering or help with event logistics.

Both sponsors are crucial for the event's success. A good combination can lead to a better overall experience for attendees, which can mean a higher chance of the event's success.

Throughout my journey of approaching sponsors, the phrase "beggars can't be choosers" resonated with me. I was grateful for any support, despite my disadvantaged position. I embraced the opportunities with appreciation, working tirelessly to create value for our sponsors.

Although I didn't have any cash sponsors at hand, I went ahead with the event. Having only secured in-kind sponsors for this concert, it was my duty to ensure these sponsors got the most out of their resources. I prominently featured their logos on event materials, granted them access to VIP areas, and invited them to the press release. My sponsors saw my commitment to delivering value in return for their support.

My early years as a business owner taught me valuable lessons that have shaped my approach to event planning. I realised the difference between a wonderful event and a successful event. My intuition was important for overcoming challenges. I grasped the need to balance talks and take action to prevent missed chances. Effective time management, delegation, and finding alternative solutions were key to overcoming obstacles. These lessons paved the way for my overall growth as a business owner and event planner.

THE DAY I LOST

EMBRACING LIFE LESSONS AS AN EVENT MANAGEMENT START-UP

"God lets everything happen for a reason. It's all a learning process, and you have to go from one level to another."

– Mike Tyson

On the day before the event, our emotions were askew. We felt a mix of excitement, nervousness, and anticipation. We had invested so much time and effort into making this concert a reality, and now everything was coming together.

Reflecting on the journey leading up to this point, we acknowledged the challenges we had faced. The brainstorming sessions, the meticulous planning and the budgeting had all tested our abilities. But we persevered, fuelled by our determination to create something extraordinary.

With each passing hour, our excitement grew. We could feel the energy building up, both within ourselves and among the team. The sleepless nights and long days had been worth it. We had poured our hearts into every detail, ensuring that everything was as perfect as possible.

Success was determined not only by logistics but also by the impression we left on attendees. Our hope was for the concert to be a memorable experience for all attendees. We were eager to receive feedback, learn from it and make improvements in future events.

With each passing hour, our anticipation grew. We double-checked every arrangement, confirmed payments, and made sure everything was in order. We wanted the day to go smoothly, with no hiccups or unexpected surprises.

Although we still had some jitters, we were ready to embrace the unknown. We knew that no matter how meticulously we had planned, there would always be some unpredictability. And that's what made events like these so special—the magic that unfolded in the moment.

As we prepared for the day, we held a sense of fulfilment in our hearts. We had given it our all, and now it was time to witness the result of our efforts. We were proud of what we had achieved and were excited to see the reactions of the audience.

THE TURNING POINT: DAY OF THE EVENT

As the morning sun bathed the sky in vibrant shades, it felt like a beautiful hint, a sign that today would be a remarkable day. The colours painted across the horizon mirrored the excitement and anticipation that filled the air. It was as if the sky itself was setting the stage for the joy and energy that awaited inside the venue.

From the early hours of the morning, my team and I were already hard at work. The final touches were being added, ensuring that every aspect of the event was flawless. As I looked around the venue, a swell of pride washed over me. The transformation was remarkable. Every piece of equipment, every prop, and every material had been meticulously arranged. It was evidence of the dedication and effort we had poured into every single detail. From the stage setup to the lighting design, no aspect had been overlooked.

The stage stood tall and ready, beckoning performers to step into the spotlight. The seating arrangements were meticulously placed, ensuring optimal views and comfort for the attendees. Every corner of the venue had been thoughtfully curated to create an atmosphere that would leave a lasting impression. We were ready to welcome them, to create an experience that would be fixed in their memories forever.

RISING WORRIES: BUILDING TENSION BEFORE THE EVENT

As the time for the event had almost arrived, a sense of uneasiness crept in. The realisation that only a few tickets had been sold and there were no cash sponsors for the event weighed heavily on my mind. It felt like a daunting challenge, and uncertainty loomed over the success of the event.

However, I refused to let these worries consume me. To calm my nerves and regain a sense of composure, I turned to the power of visualisation. I closed my eyes and allowed my imagination to paint a vivid picture of a flawless event. I saw myself standing confidently on stage, delivering a captivating performance or speech to an enthralled audience. This mental exercise helped me regain my self-assurance and reminded me of the immense potential for success that still lay ahead.

During moments of doubt, I sought support and encouragement from my trusted team and colleagues. Their unwavering support and belief in me was a source of strength. The comfort I received reminded me we were all on this journey together and had a common goal we were working towards. Their collective energy and dedication provided the motivation I needed to keep pushing forward.

I understood that setbacks and challenges were a part of any attempt, and it was essential to remain tough and persistent. I reminded myself that setbacks were opportunities for growth and learning. Even in the face of difficulty, I held onto my love for what I was doing and my unwavering commitment to its success.

With a renewed sense of determination and a support system by my side, I found the strength to face my worries head-on. I knew I couldn't control every outcome, but I could control my attitude and effort. I would give it my all until the very end, trusting that my hard work and passion would pave the way for success.

THE LAST HOUR: THE CALM BEFORE THE STORM

As the event was ready to begin, I witnessed the incredible strength of teamwork and collaboration. The initial nervousness that had lingered in the back of my mind was replaced with fulfilment and joy. The concerns about limited ticket sales and the absence of sponsors faded away in the face of the incredible experience we had created.

Attendees embraced the event with enthusiasm and energy. As soon as they arrived, they were delighted and engaged with what we had planned. The atmosphere buzzed with positivity and anticipation, making the event truly come alive.

Amidst the excitement, I remained focused on staying organised. Every minor detail mattered, as even the slightest oversight could disrupt the flow of the event.

The mounting pressure was undeniable, but I refused to let it overwhelm me. I maintained composure and focused on each task at hand. Deep breaths helped to calm my nerves and provided a moment of respite amidst the whirlwind of activity.

WHEN FEARS COME TRUE: DEALING WITH DISAPPOINTMENT FROM LOW TURNOUT

The anxiety came in waves. It was time to begin, and the nagging doubts crept in yet again. Had I done enough to promote the event? Would people show up and appreciate the hard work I had put into organising it?

The weight of anticipation bore down heavily on my shoulders. It was disheartening to imagine empty seats in the venue, serving as a severe reminder of the lack of interest or support for the event. In those crucial moments, it was hard to shake off the sense of disappointment that loomed overhead. The thoughts of low attendance created a sense of self-doubt, making me question the value and appeal of the event. It felt like a personal rejection, undermining my confidence and passion.

As the event approached, I had to confront the reality of the situation. I had to come to terms with the possibility of a smaller turnout than expected. It was a bitter pill to swallow as I grappled with feelings of inadequacy and frustration.

In times like these, it's essential to remember that low turnout does not define the quality of the event or the worth of my efforts. It's important to resist the temptation to blame myself or overanalyzed what went wrong. Setbacks happen, and it's crucial to view them as learning experiences rather than personal failures.

Though the disappointment of low attendance stung, I vowed to use it as a motivation for future endeavours. I would reevaluate my promotional strategies and consider alternative approaches. This setback would serve as a reminder of the importance of adaptability and spirit in the face of difficulty.

As the event was about to begin, I remained positive and focused. I would greet each attendee with gratitude and enthusiasm, regardless of the turnout. I would strive to deliver a memorable experience to those who came, recognising that their presence was a testament to their interest and support.

In the end, it's crucial to persevere and not let the fear of low attendance overshadow our passion and drive. Setbacks can sometimes lead to success.

Dealing with Unexpected Problems: Handling Unexpected Payment Requests from Suppliers

As the event drew to a close, I felt increasing stress when suppliers started asking for their payment.

They complained about their security and were hesitant to take risks because of the low attendance at the event, but I assured them I would resolve the financial issue quickly.

To show my commitment and build trust, I made a partial payment right away. This showed them I was serious about fulfilling my financial commitments. I also requested a clear timeline for when I could make the remaining payment in full. This helped set expectations and conveyed to them I was taking their concerns seriously.

Fortunately, my suppliers were understanding and had faith in me. I felt a sense of relief when I realised how supportive they were and how much they trusted my abilities.

Their confidence in me made me realise the importance of building and maintaining trust. Paying suppliers promptly was necessary to uphold my reputation and credibility in the market. Building an excellent reputation with suppliers and fulfilling my commitments could help me stand out in the business world. Honoring my promises was essential for my long-term success.

Despite the disappointment of low attendance, it's important to remember that setbacks happen to everyone. It's how we respond to these setbacks that truly define us. While the low turnout was disheartening, I found the silver lining in the situation. I analysed what went wrong, sought feedback from attendees and brainstormed ways to improve for future events.

In the end, even though my worst fears became a reality, I didn't allow them to define me. In moments when life throws you off balance, it's important to find something that helps get you back up and keep moving forward. For me, that something was dancing.

Dancing became a source of empowerment and positivity. It allowed me to let loose and immerse myself in the rhythm. It diverted my attention from the negative aspects and embrace a more optimistic mindset. Whether it was dancing with my team, colleagues, friends, or family, it created a sense of unity and camaraderie that lifted our spirits.

OVERCOMING SADNESS AND FINDING HOPE

I suddenly found myself on the brink of ruin, uncertain of which way to turn. It felt like everything was going wrong and hope seemed distant. I carried the weight of my responsibilities and fears, and the future seemed bleak.

Income levels are subjective to each person. Imagine if someone making Dhs 1,500 per month lost Dhs 150,000, it would drastically change their life. In contrast, someone earning Dhs 15,000 per month might be less affected because of their ability to recover the same amount in less than a year. Losing over Dhs 150,000 on one concert was a substantial setback in the initial stages of my company, as we were just beginning to establish ourselves in the industry. Building back up from rock bottom seemed like an impossible task.

During this darkness, a flicker of determination sparked within me. I refused to let this situation define me. I set out to explore distinct possibilities and options to rebuild.

REFLECTING ON THE EVENT AND FINDING A WAY FORWARD

I was alone at the venue, thinking back on the event while my team took down the setup. The weight of my financial responsibilities towards suppliers and artists overwhelmed me. Instead of dwelling on the negatives, I focused on seeking solutions. I began devising a plan to repay my debts and reassess my strategies for future events.

Now, it was time to reinvent my approach, incorporating the lessons I had learned and making necessary adjustments. I needed to think creatively and explore new strategies that would enable me to navigate future events more effectively.

DIFFERENTIATING BETWEEN A GOOD EVENT AND A SUCCESSFUL EVENT

Differentiating between a good event and a successful event was a crucial step for me in refining my goals and strategies for future events. Through careful analysis, I gained a clearer understanding of what distinguishes the two.

A "good" event focuses on creating a positive and memorable experience for attendees. This involves delivering entertainment, ensuring satisfaction, and providing value for the price of admission. A wonderful event leaves attendees with enjoyable memories and a sense of fulfilment.

A "successful" event goes beyond just being good. It involves achieving specific objectives and measurable outcomes. Generating a profit, financial balance, or attaining a ticket sales goal. A successful event is one that not only leaves attendees satisfied but also achieves the desired outcomes set by the organisers.

Reflecting on my event, I realised it had met the criteria of being a good event in terms of creating a positive experience for attendees. However, it failed to meet the criteria for success because goals like attendance and revenue weren't reached.

This realisation prompted me to set more specific and measurable goals for future events. A successful event requires clear objectives and plans that support them by refining my marketing and promotion, exploring alternative revenue sources, and constantly evaluating my approach.

EMBRACING CHANGE
TO ACHIEVE SUCCESS!

"When things are bad, it's the best time to reinvent yourself."

– George Lopez

I took a step back after the concert. I reevaluated my strategies and designed new, attainable goals with one purpose in mind: to reshape my destiny.

Until this point, I was predominantly managing artists and booking them for shows. But after organising the concert, I realised I had a talent for planning events. This inspired me to diversify my business into event management, production, and rentals. Expanding would give me a wider client base and a steady income, which I needed to pay my suppliers and cover expenses.

To kick start this expansion, I invested in professional speakers that I could rent out to clients along with the entertainers they were booking through me. This idea was well-received because clients no longer had to hire a separate vendor. They could get everything they needed in one package.

Investing in high-quality equipment, such as professional speakers, was a smart move. It guaranteed proper functionality and optimal sound quality. My complete entertainment and sound equipment package made me gain an enormous advantage in the industry. It made hosting events easier. This led to increased customer satisfaction, repeat business, and heaps of word-of-mouth referrals. These packages slowly helped me build a solid base for steady income.

Interestingly, to date, I still have the first speakers I invested in. They serve as a symbol of the dedication that went into rebuilding my company. Holding onto this equipment reminds me of my journey and the principles that helped me succeed.

FIRST THINGS FIRST! FULFILLING COMMITMENTS: PAYING SUPPLIERS & ARTISTS.

I remained fully committed to my promise of paying my suppliers and artists. Repaying them became my top priority after the concert. Keeping up with my payments ensured suppliers were satisfied and my reputation stayed positive. Timely payments to entertainers and suppliers must be a priority in this field. This not only strengthens relationships, but also builds a reputation for reliability and trustworthiness. Vendors also provide better service if they trust you. By avoiding delayed payments, you reduce stress and maintain the quality of your work, leading to overall business success.

REFLECT AND ACT SWIFTLY: NAVIGATING DECISIVE STEPS

Once I sorted out my financial responsibilities, I needed to dig deep about the mistakes I was making. Questions haunted my mind. Who or what was to blame? Did I make a defective plan, choose the wrong options, or fail in my execution?

As the pieces of the puzzle slowly fell into place, I saw the bigger picture. The key to sorting out the mysteries lay in three fundamental aspects: who, what, and why. I needed to identify the people involved in this unfortunate turn of events, the actions they took, and the reasons behind them. By examining these elements, I could shed light on the series of events that led to the concert's failure.

First, the "who" aspect came into focus. I realized that one of the key factors contributing to the event's losses was the decision to fully rely on a freelance sponsorship partner. This choice led to missed opportunities, particularly in securing cash sponsors independently. Recognizing this, I understood that diversifying my approach and not placing all my eggs in one basket would have allowed me to tap into additional resources, potentially mitigating the loss.

Second, the "what" factor became apparent. Until that point, my expertise primarily revolved around managing artists and booking them for shows. Organizing and executing an event was a new territory for me.

Last, the "why" element shed light on another critical lesson. The importance of meticulous planning became clear, especially to select the right date, day and venue for the event. This insight underscored the need to consider the event's uniqueness, target audience, and potential competition. Avoiding overlapping events on the same day was essential to ensure an undivided crowd.

By examining these three aspects–who, what, and why–I gained valuable insights into the factors that contributed to the event's challenges. This introspection not only helped me understand the root causes but also empowered me with knowledge to make informed decisions in the future. It was a turning point that propelled me towards growth and resilience.

BY INCORPORATING THE THREE W'S - WHO, WHAT AND WHY

Now that I had organised a concert, I realised there was a much wider audience I could target. I started offering corporate events, hotel promotions, and mall promotions. This diversification allowed me to reach new markets and made my business more adaptable and sustainable.

I transitioned from a laid-back approach to an action-oriented mindset. I defined my target clients, studied my competitors that were slowly emerging in the market, and learned from their practices. I also established key relationships with suppliers and partners crucial for success in the industry.

I determined the range of services and products I could offer and developed a unique value proposition. I created a pricing strategy and set clear short-term and long-term business goals.

Understanding the demand for my services and products was crucial. I highlighted the reasons customers should choose my business over competitors. This helped me identify potential challenges and opportunities in the industry.

By adopting this structured approach and maintaining an action-oriented mindset, I continuously adapted to meet the evolving needs of clients, which was essential to being a top player in the market.

LOSS IS GAIN

TURNING SETBACKS INTO SUCCESS

"One gains by losing and loses by gaining."

– Lao Tzu, Tao Te Ching

When I experienced loss, it felt tough. I had put in a lot of effort and dedication, so it made me feel useless and wonder why I had to lose.

To cope with the loss, I realised I needed to find activities that brought me joy and made me feel good. One of the best ways to lift my mood was to spend time with my two wonderful daughters. Their love and presence helped me feel better and gave me a sense of purpose.

I also attempted to change my view about the event. Instead of thinking about what I had lost, I started focusing on the positive aspects of the experience I gained. I looked for silver linings and tried to see the potential opportunities that might come my way in the future.

It wasn't easy, but I reminded myself to let go of the past and look ahead. I believed in the saying, "Whatever happens, happens for the best". This mindset helped me find hope and courage to keep moving forward.

Instead of getting into a dark space focusing on how much money I had lost, I switched my attention to creating new business prospects. I reached out to people in my network and actively searched for potential clients. Even though it required faxing and making many calls, I attempted to connect with them. To my luck, opportunities to handle events came sooner than expected. I received calls from corporate clients and hotels, asking me to organise full scale events.

Every success we achieved in handling events became a reason to celebrate. We took time to acknowledge our achievements, which helped us stay motivated and build confidence for future opportunities.

TURNING FAILURES INTO STEPPING STONES TO SUCCESS

I often wondered what would have happened if my first concert had been profitable. It might have tempted me to organise more and bigger concerts, which could have led to an even bigger loss. Instead, I focused on becoming an event planner specialising in corporate events. I learned from my experiences and understood the importance of having a sustainable business model with minimised risks.

EVERY CLOUD HAS A SILVER LINING

This saying suggests that even during difficult times, there is often a positive aspect or outcome to be found. It motivates us to find the positive aspect or the potential opportunities that can result from hardship. The subject is centered around discovering hope and confidence during difficult times, with the belief that something good can arise from a negative situation. This serves as a reminder to always maintain a positive outlook and actively seek opportunities for personal growth and improvement, especially during times of difficulty.

I started to believe in myself and my abilities. It all began with having a clear idea of what I wanted to achieve and setting goals that matched that vision. Once I had my goals in place, I made sure to stay focused and motivated, even when faced with challenges and setbacks.

I understood that success in business wasn't just about making money. It was also about making a positive impact on my customers, employees, and the community. I stayed true to my values and beliefs, and I always remembered my purpose and passion for what I was doing. By doing all of this, I knew I could create a business that was not only successful but also meaningful.

A KIDS BIRTHDAY PARTY
THAT SHAPED MY THINKING

"A pessimist sees the difficulty in every opportunity; an optimist sees the opportunity in every difficulty."

– Winston Churchill

After going through the 'Who, What, Why' questions and restructuring our process and plans after the concert, I clearly remember the day at the office when my partner and I sat down to discuss our survival strategy for the upcoming months. It was a critical moment as we struggled with the challenges ahead and brainstormed ideas to keep our business afloat. We were determined to pull through and ensure our survival in the face of difficulty.

After facing a significant setback with our event, we realized the urgency of the situation. Our company's future was at stake, and we had to act swiftly. Failure was not an option.

We focused on generating income by any means necessary. We brainstormed ideas and explored new possibilities. Every decision we made was driven by our unwavering goal of securing our financial well-being. The pressure was immense, but it fuelled our determination. We were prepared to go to great lengths, take calculated risks, and push ourselves beyond our limits. We couldn't afford to fail; the stakes were too high.

In the midst of figuring out our next steps, a call interrupted us. At first, I was skeptical, wondering if it was a prank or a hoax. However, I continued the conversation cautiously.

The caller inquired about our services, asking us if they could book clowns. Then, they asked about jugglers, face painters, and stilt walkers. I kept saying "yes" as he went through the list. We had it all. However, I still doubted if the call was a prank as it was a long list and I was not in the mood to waste time.

We were already under pressure to clear payments we had promised to our suppliers. Time was of the essence, and we didn't have the liberty to waste it. Little did I know that this call would play a significant role in our journey. Despite my initial doubts, we took a chance and explored this unexpected lead. We understood that time was money, but we also recognized the value of seizing opportunities when they arise.

I was almost inclined to hang up after the caller told us the theme after going through his entire list. He asked us to plan a Disneyland-themed event.

While it may not sound too absurd now, at that point, it was something we had never come across before. To gather more information, I started asking him some basic questions. I inquired about their name, location, and the name of their company. He mentioned we should come to their office, which provided some reassurance.

We visited their office, and my gut feeling told me that this could be a promising opportunity for us. Once we presented our company, they gave us the entire list of what was on their mind. Along with what they mentioned on the call, they also wanted candy floss stands, costume characters, magicians, a mini train and balloon decorations. It was overwhelming because we weren't accustomed to working with such additional requirements. The biggest shock came towards the end of the meeting. They wanted everything in two days.

I hadn't asked about the event date over the phone, and it turned out to be a blessing in disguise. If they had initially mentioned the tight timeframe, I might have refused because of the scale of the requirements.

While talking to the client, two things were running through my mind: the need for money and the opportunity to make or break our business. I informed the client that I would check availability and get back to them the next morning. We returned to the office and immediately started making calls.

Fortunately, most of the responses were positive, and we secured availability and pricing.

Within 3-4 hours, we gathered all the information. I phoned the client, gave them our proposal, and explained we needed payment because of limited funds. They agreed and requested us to collect the money from their office the next morning.

We arrived at the client's office by 9 am, collected the advance payment, discussed a few details, and set off to execute our plans. Throughout the day, our focus was on taking action and ensuring that everything we promised was in place. Working with most of the suppliers for the first time, we relied on trust and built relationships with them.

After a tiring day of planning and preparation, we were ready to make our large-scale event a success. Despite the challenges of handling such an event for the first time, our determination to leave a lasting impact kept us going.

Finally, the event day arrived, scheduled to begin at 4 pm. With roughly 8 hours to set up, we started early in the morning at the beautiful outdoor lawn venue, which perfectly matched our theme.

We worked tirelessly, paying attention to every detail, ensuring a flawless execution. There was no room for mistakes and we left nothing to chance. The hours flew by as we hustled to bring our vision to life. We embraced the pressure and worked tirelessly to ensure that everything ran smoothly.

By the time the event started, we were confident that our hard work had paid off. The venue looked stunning; the atmosphere was electric, and we knew we had delivered on our promise.

I can still picture the day. Bright colors all around, balloons, character meet-and-greets, and a mini train adding a special touch. Popcorn and candy floss machines were set up at different corners. Magicians, stilt-walkers, and jugglers added to the festive atmosphere, bringing the Disneyland experience to life.

It was fulfilling, knowing that we had surpassed our expectations and created an event to remember. The exhaustion was worth it, and we were proud of the seamless execution.

This event was a valuable learning opportunity, and it further fuelled our passion for event planning. We were ready to take on new challenges, armed with the knowledge that our determination and attention to detail would lead to success.

We were thrilled that our team could create a fun and memorable experience. After successfully completing the event and receiving full payment, we felt a sense of relief and released the stress that had been weighing us down. This experience reinforced the idea that maintaining a positive mindset is crucial. When we think positively and believe in our abilities, it becomes easier to overcome challenges and achieve our goals. It felt like a miracle had happened to us. We were in the right place at the right time, and it motivated us to plan for the future and continue making things happen.

THINK LIKE A TRAFFIC SIGNAL

MASTERING CONTROL AND DIRECTION IN LIFE

"Action without planning is the cause of all failure. Action with planning is the cause of all success."

– Brian Tracy

One of the most valuable lessons I have learnt on my own is to "think like a traffic signal". Seems strange? Let's dig a little deeper.

A traffic signal serves as a symbol of control and direction on the roads. Just like a traffic signal, we can apply its principles to our own lives, enabling us to navigate through the complications and make sound decisions.

Stop: The red signal teaches us the importance of pausing and taking a moment to review our situations. Sometimes, it's necessary to hit the brakes, to stop and reflect. By slowing down and evaluating our circumstances, we can avoid rash actions and make more knowledgeable choices.

Wait: The yellow signal reminds us of the value of patience and caution. It signifies a moment of hesitation, urging us to wait for the right opportunity or to gather more information before moving forward. Just as we wait for the signal to turn green, exercising patience allows us to make better judgments and avoid unnecessary risks.

Go: The green signal represents action and progress. It encourages us to move forward, seize opportunities, and embrace new experiences. When we think like a green signal, we develop a positive mindset, taking the steps to achieve our goals and ambitions.

Thinking like a traffic signal involves mastering the art of balance and decision-making. It teaches us to recognise when to stop and reflect, when to exercise patience and when to take bold action. By incorporating these principles into our lives, we can achieve a sense of control, clarity, and direction.

When faced with challenging situations, we can ask ourselves: Do I need to stop and re-evaluate? Should I exercise patience and gather more information? Or is it time to take the leap and move forward?

By thinking like a traffic signal, we become more mindful of our choices and actions. We learn to navigate the difficulties of life with greater ease and confidence. Just as a traffic signal guides and directs the flow of vehicles, embracing this mindset enables us to navigate the twists and turns of life's journey, ensuring that we reach our desired destinations with clarity and purpose.

Thinking like a traffic signal has taught me valuable lessons, and there are three reasons it's so impactful.

First, traffic signals are everywhere in our daily lives. We see them everywhere out on the road. Their presence is constant, making them relatable and easy to apply to our own lives.

Second, thinking like a traffic signal is a simple yet powerful reminder. The traffic signal reminds us naturally, with no extra effort or resources. Whenever we come across a traffic signal or wait at one, it reminds us to pause, reflect, and take action.

But the most important aspect of thinking, like a traffic signal, is its ability to prompt us to act on our thoughts. Traffic signals regulate traffic, ensuring a smooth and safe flow of vehicles. When we adopt the mindset of a traffic signal, it motivates us to take decisive action based on our thoughts and intentions. It encourages us to be active rather than passive, engaging with our ideas and pursuing our goals.

A traffic signal can symbolise our thoughts and help us stay on track. It helps us navigate life with clarity, purpose, and momentum. A traffic signal can help us progress towards our goals.

HOW A TRAFFIC SIGNAL RESEMBLES OUR MIND

Traffic signals are controlled by a system that manages the timing of lights to make traffic flow smoothly. Similarly, our mind should act as a central controller for our plans and goals, ensuring that our thoughts and actions align with what we want to achieve.

In business, it's crucial to understand our objectives and create a plan to reach them. By having a centralised plan, we can make sure that our actions are in line with our goals and keep us on the right path.

However, it's also important to be adaptable. We should adjust our plans and strategies when needed. This flexibility allows us to stay on track and achieve our goals, even in the face of unexpected challenges.

DIFFERENT APPROACHES TO TURNING THOUGHTS INTO ACTION

Some people have many ideas but struggle to put them into action. This can be because they fear failure, lack confidence in themselves, or they have a habit of thinking and dreaming without taking action. Then there are those who are go-getters. They not only think and plan but also take action on their thoughts and ideas.

Launching and running a successful business requires more than just having an idea. It takes hard work and determination to turn an idea into a profitable venture. If you have a business idea that you're passionate about, it's important to bring it to life. Seeking help from experts can be beneficial.

It's important to understand that both thinking and action are necessary for success. While having ideas is important, taking action is what leads to progress and achievement. By combining strategic thinking with purposeful action, individuals can overcome their barriers and increase their chances of success.

THE THREE TYPES OF PEOPLE IN BUSINESS

In my opinion, there are three distinct types of individuals when it comes to doing business. Let's explore each group:

Cautious: These individuals prefer to avoid risks in business. They are more comfortable with stability and may hesitate to make significant changes or take on new challenges.

Risk-Taker: This group embraces risks in business, driven by the potential for big rewards. They will take bold actions, fuelled by their passion for innovation and their desire to create something new.

Calculated Risk-Taker: A third group falls in between, taking calculated risks based on careful analysis and evaluation of potential outcomes. They rely on data, market research, and other forms of analysis to inform their decisions.

Understanding which group you belong to is crucial for making sound decisions in your business. If you are cautious, you may need to push yourself out of your comfort zone to achieve greater success. If you are a risk-taker, you may need to consider the potential consequences of your actions. And if you are a calculated risk-taker, strive for a balance between caution and recklessness in decision-making. Recognising your risk tolerance and developing strategies to manage risk can help you achieve success in business.

Think it, plan it, do it - Focus on the Process, Results Will Follow

To achieve success, it's important to focus on the process rather than just the end results. The mantra of "Think it, plan it, do it" guides us in laying a firm foundation for achieving our goals.

It starts with thinking. We generate ideas, clarify our objectives, and explore different perspectives. This helps us evaluate challenges and figure out the steps to move forward.

Once we have a clear idea, we plan. We break down our goal into actionable steps, create a timeline, and allocate resources effectively. Planning gives us direction, focus, and organization.

But it doesn't stop there—we must take action. Doing is where progress happens. We commit, work hard, and overcome challenges. By turning our plans into actions, we make genuine progress toward our goals.

While results matter, success comes from focusing on the process. By dedicating ourselves to thinking, planning, and doing, we set ourselves up for success. This approach builds momentum, allows us to learn from experiences, and make necessary adjustments.

Focusing on the process helps us develop valuable skills, gain knowledge, and cultivate a growth mindset. It encourages us to see challenges as opportunities for learning and improvement. Even if immediate results fall short, the skills, insights, and spirit we gain contribute to long-term success.

QUICK THINKING THAT SAVED US

USING THE TRAFFIC SIGNAL FORMULA

"We are supposed to think and act, in contrary we act and think."

– Lisa Roy

We had just finished with a setup with one of our regular hotel clients. They were hosting the annual Ramadan event outdoors that required entertainment, sound, and lights. For this particular setup, they had an additional requirement of something we don't usually provide: outdoor furniture. This happened to be a last-minute request that cropped up because their supplier backed out. Being committed event planners, we couldn't turn down such a significant task. We needed to deliver a large quantity of furniture, which was almost around 300 coffee tables with sofas of 3+2 seating within a tight timeframe, which we pulled off.

After the festive season, people usually reign in the celebrations during the first few months of the year. With fewer events around this time, we found ourselves with some free time on our hands, and so we set off on a short trip to Oman.

JOURNEY INTERRUPTED: AN UNEXPECTED CALL AMIDST OUR DRIVE

As we were on the road between Dubai and Muscat, we received an unexpected call. The hotel required us to clear their outdoor furniture within two days for an upcoming cultural event. This caught us by surprise as we hadn't planned where to store the furniture, and we had limited space. We felt a mix of panic and confusion about tackling this significant job. The confusion arose from a misunderstanding–we thought the hotel had purchased the furniture, but they had actually rented it, similar to the sound and lights setup.

We suggested that since they had purchased the furniture instead of renting it, they could handle its disposal themselves. But the hotelier was adamant, demanding that we clear it without delay.

We faced two dilemmas: First; we wanted to support our loyal client and ensure this issue wouldn't affect our overall working relationship. Second, we needed to find a solution that wouldn't cause any losses for ourselves or inconvenience to those involved.

FINDING CALM AMIDST STRESS

Our enhanced intelligence was clear this time as we learned from our previous errors. Our decision was to implement the traffic signal formula. We decided to take a much-needed tea break to clear our minds. This ritual always brought us mental clarity. It was during this tea break that an ingenious idea struck us.

We proposed the idea of temporarily storing the furniture at our sponsor's house, as it seemed like the only viable option at the time. However, convincing our sponsor to agree to this arrangement became our next challenge. Through negotiations and persuasion, we struck a deal, and our sponsor graciously agreed to accommodate our request.

This breakthrough revitalised our spirits, knowing that we had found a workable solution. We had managed to solve one of our two dilemmas. We could now focus on meeting our client's needs, with the storage issue resolved. The furniture would be safe until a suitable long-term arrangement could be made. Having informed our team to transport the furniture to our sponsor's house, we continued our journey to Oman with a sigh of relief.

SHORT-LIVED SERENITY: A TEMPORARY RESPITE FROM CHALLENGES

Our sense of relief was short-lived as we received another call a few hours later. It was our sponsor, expressing his dissatisfaction and shock regarding the quantity of furniture. His house was filled to the brim, making it difficult to move around comfortably. They insisted we clear the furniture by the next day.

This fresh development posed a significant challenge. We felt a great responsibility to find a solution and not disappoint our sponsor. With time rapidly running out, we knew we had to act swiftly and think outside the box. We contacted other wedding and event planning companies. We explored the possibility of selling the furniture to them while we made our way to Oman. Countless phone calls were made, and finally, a glimmer of hope appeared when we found a potential buyer interested in purchasing the furniture.

We completed the sale and planned to move the furniture, meeting both the buyer's and sponsor's expectations while also making an added profit on the furniture. All this before we even reached our mini get-away destination!

A STROKE OF LUCK: A FORTUNATE TWIST OF FATE

We were fortunate that our quick thinking worked well in our favour that day. Be ready to think on your feet and find solutions when unexpected challenges arise. When faced with the task of clearing a large amount of furniture without storage, it seemed daunting at first, but we overcame it.

JUGGLING BUSINESS

WITH JUGGLERS

"Live as if you were to die tomorrow. Learn as if you were to live forever."

– Mahatma Gandhi

During a time of great potential in the entertainment industry, I was an entrepreneur with a firm determination to make a lasting impact. The phone rang unexpectedly and to our surprise; it was the highly esteemed General Manager of a prestigious hotel on the other end of the line. During a difficult setback, this client provided me with unwavering support, which helped me get through the tough times. Because of the trust and mutual understanding that underlies our bond, this call held great significance.

As the phone rang, excitement and anticipation welled up inside me. The voice on the other end belonged to the GM, and I eagerly waited to hear what he had to say. To my surprise, his first words were a perplexing question in a stern voice that caught me off guard: "Rocky, who did you send?"

I informed him I had sent jugglers, just as he had requested. But his disappointment was clear in his voice as he repeated the question. It turned out that the entertainers I had sent were inexperienced. They could barely toss two balls in the air and catch them–a skill even the GM claimed he could do better.

A combination of sorrow and frustration overcame me, causing my heart to sink. I questioned my decision to send performers who were not up to standard. The disappointment of such a dedicated supporter like this GM hit me hard. Without any delay, I called him again and conveyed my deepest apologies, assuring him that he shouldn't bear the cost of such an unsatisfactory performance. However, he politely declined my offer, showing true character and kindness. He highlighted the need to avoid a recurrence of this incident.

In the early days of my entertainment agency, finding truly talented entertainers was an uphill battle. The market was in its infancy, talent was scarce, and we had to make do with individuals seeking a little extra pocket money. We trained them in our office, even going above and beyond by creating their costumes. Our clients, mostly emerging malls and shopping centers, sought attractions like face painters, jugglers, stilt walkers, balloon benders and magicians. Anything beyond that required importing acts from abroad.

Dealing with local entertainers was a constant challenge, as many treated their craft as a casual gig. Yet, we strived for professionalism, making punctuality and high-quality performances our top priorities. I picked up the entertainers from their homes, going to great lengths to keep them satisfied, knowing that alternatives were limited. It was a grueling battle, working within the limitations and challenges for four to five years until the industry progressed.

Looking back, while this incident now makes us laugh, it will forever be etched in my memory, serving as a stark reminder of the obstacles I faced and how it led me to focus on always providing quality service. This experience became a pivotal turning point to seek the most talented entertainers, refine our processes and elevate the reputation of my company in the industry.

TIME AND TIDE

WAITS FOR NO MAN

"It's not enough to be busy, so are the ants. The question is, what are we busy about?"

– Henry David Thoreau.

LESSONS FROM THE TIDES: EMBRACING THE VALUE OF TIME

From a young age, my father, a navy serviceman, taught me the importance of time. He compared it to the tides of the sea, emphasising that time always moves forward and waits for no one. This understanding has stayed with me throughout my life.

Growing up, my father's commitment to punctuality and his connection to the sea influenced this saying. He believed that just as the tides keep moving, time too keeps flowing. It doesn't stop or slow down, regardless of whether we are ready. This reminder urges us to make the most of our time because, once it's gone, we can't retrieve it.

These lessons shaped my perspective, instilling in me the habit of valuing and respecting time. I appreciate that time is a precious resource, and wasting it or delaying important tasks can lead to missed opportunities. It's crucial to be mindful of the passing moments and seize them to shape our future.

Reflecting on my father's wisdom, I've learned the significance of being punctual and cherishing the present. Time is a valuable asset, and by using it wisely, we can achieve our goals and fulfil our dreams.

IN MY CASE, TIME WAS MY GUIDING FORCE

In my case, time was more than just counting moments. It became very important to me and guided how I lived. I learned to be disciplined and organised because time reminded me to stay focused on my responsibilities and goals. Time also made me more aware of opportunities and encouraged me to take risks and try new things. I realised I couldn't do everything at once, so I learned to set priorities and focus on what really mattered. Time also taught me to appreciate the present moment and enjoy life's experiences. It pushed me to work hard and achieve important goals in my life. But it also reminded me to find a balance and take time for myself and my loved ones.

Time became a crucial tool for me to stand out from my competitors as an event planner and service provider. Maintaining time was not only cost-effective but also helped me attract clients who valued punctuality.

Right from the beginning, I understood the importance of time in event planning. I had the opportunity to work with 5-star hotels and resorts when I started my business. This allowed me to focus on two key aspects: time management and presenting my work professionally. I was fortunate to possess both these qualities.

It is crucial to not make excuses like traffic jams or personal issues to justify delays in maintaining time. In my early days, working with hoteliers, it was not only about maintaining time but also being ahead of time. Since I mainly worked with the Food & Beverage department and banquets, I noticed their unique working style. If we were appointed as the event planner and given a setup time of 6 PM, the F&B manager would check the venue before 6 PM to see if we were already there for the setup.

Realising the importance of punctuality and a professional setup, I made a significant change in my approach. Instead of just being on time, I started arriving at the venue well in advance. This change allowed me to enjoy the process of setting up the event, creating an atmosphere of relaxation and professionalism.

I took pleasure in being early, as it provided me with ample time to complete the setup. Arriving at least 30 minutes before the scheduled start time became a norm for me. This additional time allowed me to make any necessary last-minute adjustments and add finishing touches to enhance the overall look and feel of the event setup.

By prioritising early arrival and meticulous setup, I could ensure that everything was in place and that the event started smoothly. This approach not only instilled a sense of calm and preparedness within me, but it also left a positive impression on clients and attendees, as they could witness the attention to detail and professionalism from the very beginning.

In my daily life I have this phrase "value time and time will value you". It is very important to respect and make the most of one's time. We cannot get back once it has passed, so it is essential to use it wisely.

TIME IS MONEY: THE VALUE OF EFFECTIVE TIME MANAGEMENT IN BUSINESS

"Time is money" means that time is a valuable resource, just like money, and we should give it the same importance. It's crucial to manage our time effectively to make the most out of it. Here are some important points to keep in mind:

Prioritise tasks: Focus on the tasks that are most important and will have the biggest impact on your business.

Set deadlines: Establishing deadlines helps you stay on track and complete tasks in a timely manner.

Delegate tasks: Assign tasks to capable team members who can handle them, freeing up your time for more important work.

Monitor your time: Keep track of how you spend your time to identify any areas where you can improve and be more productive.

Effective time management brings many benefits, including increased productivity, a better work-life balance, reduced stress, improved decision-making, better customer service, increased profitability, and improved delegation of tasks.

In a highly competitive market, it's important to go beyond being a simple supplier and become a valuable team member for your clients. By focusing on providing peace of mind, collaborating for growth, and offering support beyond the basics, you can build strong relationships in the hotel industry, particularly in the F&B and banquets department. Adopting a mindset of being a team member rather than just a supplier helps you stand out from the competition and sets the foundation for long-term success and growth.

COLLABORATION
IS BETTER THAN COMPETITION

"Coming together is a beginning, staying together is progress, and working together is success."

– Henry Ford

To create more opportunities, it's important to work together as a team, form partnerships and collaborate with others. Instead of focusing on competing against each other, we should unite and work towards a common goal. Collaboration involves sharing ideas, knowledge, and resources to achieve better outcomes together.

TEAMWORK

By working as a team, we can combine our strengths and skills, leading to innovative and creative solutions. When we collaborate, we bring different perspectives and experiences to the table, helping us solve complex problems more effectively. By working together, we can access a wider range of resources and expertise, making our efforts more efficient and fruitful.

Working together with others towards a common goal is valuable. It creates a supportive and respectful environment where we can build strong relationships and trust. We provide each other with feedback, encouragement, and help, which helps us grow personally and professionally.

By embracing a mindset of teamwork and support, we establish long-term relationships. When we work together, we create a network of trusted partners who can offer future opportunities, referrals, and continued cooperation. This expands our career prospects, widens our professional connections, and opens doors to new possibilities.

Compared to fierce competition, working together offers many advantages. By valuing and respecting others, we tap into the power of collective strengths, creating better opportunities for ourselves and our partners.

From the start of my business, I believed we can all succeed without viewing others as direct competitors. Instead, I saw them as potential allies and collaborators. This mindset allowed me to highlight my unique strengths and stand out from the crowd.

This cooperative approach is crucial in today's world. When we choose to work together instead of engaging in cutthroat competition, we create amazing outcomes. It brings people and organisations together, sparks innovation and increases productivity.

During meetings with potential clients, I would confidently express that my services stand out without directly mentioning competitors. This approach protected the identities of other businesses and inspired trust in my clients regarding the quality and value I provide.

While my response may have surprised some clients, my intention was never to deny the existence of other companies. I simply focused on the value I bring and emphasised the benefits of working together.

Throughout my career, I saw others in the same industry as partners on an exciting journey. We competed professionally, striving to provide the best service without engaging in a race solely based on price.

By prioritising quality, I made a lasting impression on the market. This positive mindset influenced the professional environment I created and earned the trust and loyalty of clients who valued my commitment to delivering exceptional experiences.

It's important to see competitors as potential allies rather than enemies. When we work together and support each other, we can achieve more. Instead of trying to outdo one another, focusing on our own strengths can make us stand out. Collaboration has many advantages, like learning new things, making the most of our resources and creating a positive work environment.

LAUGHING MATTER

FINDING HUMOUR IN MY JOURNEY

"There are three ways to ultimate success: The first way is to be kind. The second way is to be kind. The third way is to be kind."

– Mister Rogers

There's something truly special about those quiet moments when I find myself alone with my thoughts. It's during these times that a rush of memories from my business journey suddenly floods my mind. It's like a series of flashbacks that transport me back to different moments in the past. These flashbacks hold a unique significance to me because they capture the spirit of my entrepreneurial experience. They remind me of the challenges I've overcome, the successes I've celebrated, and the lessons I've learned along the way. Each flashback brings a wave of emotions, from nostalgia to pride, and it's in these moments that I truly appreciate the incredible journey I've been on. These flashbacks serve as reminders of how far I've come and fuel my motivation to continue pushing forward. They are a dear part of my past, allowing me to reflect on the growth and accomplishments that have shaped my business and myself.

One of the best parts of recollecting about my past is the pure joy it brings me. The early days were tough and filled with challenges, but they were also incredibly fun and crazy.

AN UNFORGETTABLE FIRE BLOWING EXPERIENCE

Picture this: The stage is set, anticipation is in the air and our entertainer, a skilled fire blower, is ready to dazzle the guests as they arrive at our event.

When we were at the indoor venue waiting for the guests to arrive, one of my staff members went up to the entertainer and asked him to start the fire blowing show. But his response surprised us. He asked us in confusion, "Where are the guests? Who am I supposed to perform for? Should I blow fire for the plants and trees?" At that moment, we realised we were dealing with a true professional. He understood that fire blowing is an art that requires the right audience and setting. It made us appreciate his expertise and the attention he paid to every detail of his performance.

Intrigued by the entertainer's words, we engaged in a conversation to understand his perspective. It turned out that his concerns centered on safety and creating a controlled environment for his performance. We couldn't help but appreciate his commitment to the well-being of our guests, and it heightened our anticipation even more.

As time ticked away and the event unfolded with guests streaming in, we found ourselves in a state of panic. The fire blower we had hired seemed to have vanished. We frantically searched for him, realising that the moment to ignite the excitement had arrived, but he was nowhere to be found.

The situation called for immediate action, so we approached the entertainer's brother, who was there. With desperation in our voices, we pleaded with him to step in and take on the fire blowing role, even though he lacked confidence in his own abilities. We emphasised the significance of this captivating element for our event, stressing how crucial it was to create an unforgettable experience. After much persuasion, he reluctantly agreed to try it and perform some basic fire blowing. It was a moment of relief and hope amidst the chaos as we clung to the possibility of salvaging the event.

The entertainer's brother stepped up to the challenge of taking the stage. Despite lacking the expertise of his sibling, he embraced the responsibility with firm determination and delivered an impressive performance, ensuring the seamless continuation of the event.

"But where was the entertainer you hired, Rocky?" He went home to take a nap!

When we now share this story, the absurdity always makes us laugh. The story is quite captivating, allowing individuals to comprehend the unpredictability of the event industry. The contents are abundant with unexpected twists and joviality. Live experiences hold true magic in the unexpected, leaving a lasting impression on our memories.. It serves as a reminder of the exceptional essence of the industry we operate in, where unforeseeable events can occur and result in lasting memories.

There was also another, more serious lesson I had learnt. To be vigilant in choosing my entertainers wisely as their behaviour reflected on my company. While a degree of skill is definitely a priority, it is equally important to work with people you can count on.

A PECULIAR CONVERSATION: THE CHAIR RENTAL MISUNDERSTANDING

During a busy day at the office, engrossed in making calls and managing tasks, I was suddenly approached by my partner, who had a puzzled expression on his face.

A phone call had come in earlier that day, inquiring about chair rentals for an upcoming event. However, because of a series of misinterpretations, the conversation took an unexpected turn. My partner wrongly assumed the client wanted to rent a single chair. He immediately told the client we only had one chair, which was occupied.

When I was informed of this comical misunderstanding, I couldn't help but giggle at the silliness of the situation. It was a reminder that miscommunication can occur even in the simplest of inquiries and can lead to humorous consequences.

Recognising the gravity of the mistake, I took immediate action to rectify the situation. I reached out to the client, offering sincere apologies and clarifying our chair rental services for events of any size. I assured them we would go above and beyond to fulfil their specific requirements, ensuring an ample supply of chairs tailored to their needs.

This incident served as a valuable lesson, underscoring the importance of clear communication and attentiveness to our clients' needs. It highlighted the need to listen, seek clarification, and avoid making assumptions that could lead to misunderstandings and potential complications.

Through this tale of miscommunication turned comical, it is important to remember the significance of effective communication in the event management industry. It is a gentle reminder that small misunderstandings can have a significant impact, and the ability to rectify and learn from these incidents is evidence of our professionalism and dedication to our craft.

IT PAYS TO HELP OTHERS

"You can get everything in life you want if you will just help enough other people get what they want."

– Zig Ziglar

In the realm of business, I have come to appreciate the importance of going above and beyond to assist others deeply. Helping someone in need brings a profound sense of satisfaction and fulfilment. I can vividly recall three distinct occasions in my business journey where I felt an overwhelming urge to extend a helping hand.

What truly surprised me during those experiences was the realisation that offering my support not only benefited the recipients but also enriched my life in unexpected ways. It reminded me of a verse that has resonated deeply with me: "What you do unto others, you do unto me." This verse underscores the profound interconnectedness of our actions towards others, illustrating how our choices can have a profound impact not only on their lives but also on our own.

Embracing a selfless mindset opened up opportunities to help others. When we extend our help to those in need, we contribute to a cycle of kindness and compassion that brings immeasurable joy and fulfilment to both parties involved. How we treat others impacts our own experiences and can lead to positive results.

Through my experiences in helping others, I realise the profound significance of kindness and its transformative impact on the lives of individuals. It has reinforced my unwavering belief that by offering a helping hand and showing genuine care for others, we not only make a difference in their lives but also embark on a personal journey of growth, fulfilment, and purpose.

I have had the privilege of experiencing the rewards of helping others. It has opened unexpected opportunities and remarkable business ventures.

For instance, there was a time when a client required help that surpassed my usual services. Instead of turning them away, I went the extra mile to meet their needs. As a result, not only did I keep their business, but I also uncovered an entirely new opportunity in the realm of furniture rental. Witnessing how stepping up and help others can unexpectedly lead to rewards and open up new business possibilities left me awestruck.

Another memorable instance unfolded when I embraced the challenge of designing a costume for a themed party. By tapping into my creativity and honing my skills, I not only impressed my client, but also created new avenues for myself. This proved my reliability and creativity, leading to more collaborations and strong business relationships.

These examples serve as a testament to the fact that sometimes taking risks and venturing beyond our comfort zones can yield extraordinary outcomes. By prioritising the needs of our clients and showing a genuine willingness to help, we forge strong relationships and unearth new business prospects that would have otherwise remained untapped.

The concept of "positive karma" teaches us that when we selflessly assist others in expecting nothing in return, we generate positive energy that can bring unexpected benefits and opportunities into our lives. It is a reminder that our actions have a ripple effect and can shape our own experiences in both personal and professional spheres.

Hence, it is paramount to remember that while we should not always expect direct reciprocation for our actions, life has an uncanny way of rewarding us when we extend a helping hand to others. By embracing a mindset of kindness and generosity, we not only make a positive impact on the lives of others but also carve a profound path of personal growth, fulfilment and success.

THE CAREER-DEFINING EVENT

THAT SHAPED MY SUCCESS

"There's gonna be times when people tell you that you can't live your dreams. This is what I tell them, Never Say Never."

– Justin Bieber

In order to address the challenges posed by a slowdown and the need to expand our team, we dedicated a day to brainstorm ideas for growing our business. We recognised that expanding the team would come with additional costs, such as salaries and overheads, so it became crucial for us to identify strategies to generate more revenue and successfully cover these expenses.

We analysed market trends, customer preferences and target niches. It was vital for us to uncover untapped areas of growth and leverage them to propel our business forward.

Additionally, we assessed our existing operations to identify areas for improvement. We aimed to optimise processes, enhance efficiency and deliver even greater value to our customers. We refined our operations to boost customer satisfaction and loyalty.

SEIZING THE BONUS CALL FOR SUCCESS

During a busy week, I received a call from a client who wanted help with a biennial event. The event organizers had a strong desire to ensure their guests had an exceptional experience during their time in Dubai. They were determined to provide their guests with the very best, aiming to give them a fresh and positive perspective on Dubai and the Middle East. Their primary goal was to showcase the region's finest offerings, allowing their guests to truly immerse themselves in the best that Dubai offered. By delivering a remarkable experience, they hoped to challenge any previous notions about the destination and leave their guests with lasting memories and a newfound appreciation.

Ideas for this event quickly went through my mind. I assured them of my commitment to excellence and promised a prompt response.

I embarked on a quest to arrange an event that would surpass all expectations. I researched and collaborated to find the best venues, performers, and catering. Every detail was looked after to create an atmosphere of delight and wonder.

In the following days, creativity and thorough planning took center stage. By consulting with industry experts, exploring innovative technologies and implementing imaginative strategies, we were able to produce an exceptional event. We worked tirelessly to craft an experience that would leave a lasting impression on every attendee.

When my client reviewed the proposal, they were highly impressed and immediately confirmed it. This marked a significant milestone in my business, as the potential billing and profits were substantial.

This event gave us the chance to showcase our commitment to excellence. We went above and beyond, redefining what it meant to deliver the best. Every decision and detail were carefully considered and crafted with utmost care.

GOING ABOVE AND BEYOND TO EXCEED EXPECTATIONS

We pulled all the strings right from the beginning. We transferred our guests from the airport to their hotel in limousines. Picture guests arriving in sleek and stylish limousines, chauffeured by professionals. Inside, they would discover plush leather seats, state-of-the-art sound systems and climate control. It's the essence of a hassle-free and luxurious start or end to any trip.

LUXURY STAY

All our guests were booked at a luxurious resort in Palm Jumeirah, its picturesque setting overlooking of the Arabian

Gulf. Our goal was to provide every esteemed guest with a lavish and indulgent stay throughout the event. By making a strategic choice, we were able to give our guests a sense of tranquility and allow them to fully experience the captivating beauty of Dubai's coastline.

Our attendees were catered to with a wide array of sophisticated amenities at the chosen luxurious resort. Every detail was meticulously attended to, from personalized concierge services to elegantly furnished suites. Our guests relaxed in style with the resort's spa and beach. We created a luxurious atmosphere and provided impeccable service to give our guests a memorable stay that evokes the grandeur of Dubai.

7 STAR GALA DINNER

For a truly extraordinary evening, we hosted a gala dinner at a remarkable 7-star resort. The dinner unfolded in a beautifully adorned ballroom. Exquisite floral arrangements, sparkling chandeliers and elegant table settings set the tone for the night. The top chefs crafted a gourmet feast featuring a diverse selection of international and local delicacies.

To heighten the dining experience, we supplied a jazz band and talented entertainers. The smooth melodies of the jazz band set a relaxed and refined atmosphere, performing popular tunes and timeless jazz standards. The combination of fine dining, live music, and enchanting performances created a complete sensory experience, leaving a lasting impression on all attendees.

LUXURY CRUISE

When day 2 came around, we look our guests on a cruise experience that would truly stand out from the rest. Tall glass-walls, live piano accompaniment and a high-end dining experience where each course would be a work of art made our guests immerse themselves into an all-encompassing luxury experience that would create memories to treasure.

DESERT SAFARI

To capture the essence of Arabian hospitality, we took our guests on a desert safari adventure. They could explore the desert with camel riding, dune bashing, sand boarding, and falconry. Imagine the unique perspective gained from a serene camel ride across the desert landscape. To enhance the Arabian experience, a traditional Bedouin-style dinner was served in a desert camp, complete with aromatic Arabic coffee, delicious dates and flavourful local dishes. Live music performances, mesmerising dance displays, and other captivating forms of entertainment enriched the evening, creating an unforgettable journey into the heart of Arabian culture.

SIGHTSEEING & SHOPPING

Last, we organised shopping trips, visits and tours for spouses during events or conferences. This ensured that all attendees, including spouses, had a positive experience. The trips included visits to high-end boutiques, local markets and shopping centres, allowing spouses to purchase souvenirs or luxury items.

The successful outcome of the three-day event confirmed the sincerity of our tagline, "Think of an event, we make it happen" and showed our expertise in getting the job done, no matter how small or big.

ELEVATING YOUR BRAND: THE SIGNIFICANCE AND BENEFITS OF PARTICIPATING IN EXHIBITIONS

As I reflect on my experiences, one key aspect that truly stands out is the immense value of participating in exhibitions for businesses. It's a super effective way to get noticed and become more visible in the market. This lavish career-defining event was from someone who discovered us at an exhibition – it really changed the game for us. It made me realize just how something as trivial as attending an exhibition can help in reaching out to potential clients and creating fresh business opportunities.

Exhibitions present a prime opportunity to display our products or services to an audience that is genuinely interested. It's not just about showcasing what we've got–it's about making connections with experts in the field and having genuine conversations with the exact people we want to reach. Plus, it's a way to differ from our competitors, get our brand out there, and leave a mark that sticks.

The personal interactions at exhibitions are truly remarkable. It presents us with the chance to meet individuals in person and converse about our respective endeavors. This is a much more effective method compared to sending emails or posting online. And when we do this, we can explain what makes us special and why people should care about us.

Being part of exhibitions also helps us find new clients who might not have found us otherwise. It's like opening up doors to meet people who are interested in what we offer. And it's not just about clients–it's also about meeting other businesses to team up with or learn from. It's possible for us to determine the latest trends, consumer interests and the strategies of our competitors.

Exhibitions allow us to display our excellence. Captivating booths, engaging talks, and informative brochures can help us become leaders and win the trust of our audience.. It's like saying, "Hey, we know our stuff, and we're super creative and smart."

So, when you think about it, exhibitions are like a secret weapon in our plan to get more clients and grow our business. These exhibitions are like a major piece of our marketing puzzle, helping us make the most out of every opportunity and zooming ahead with our business dreams..

IF YOU DREAM IT

YOU CAN DO IT

"It does not cost to dream, Keep dreaming, but action your dreams."

– Roque Quadros

It does not cost to dream. Keep dreaming, but don't forget to action your dreams.

Dreaming is vital for all of us, as it sparks possibilities and ignites creativity. Everything in life starts with a dream, and without dreams, the world would be unrecognisable. The best part is that dreaming costs nothing–it's a gift we all have.

Dreams transport our minds to a wonderful world of fantastic scenes and innovative ideas. However, to make dreams come true, taking action is crucial. Countless ideas remain unrealised due to a lack of action, missing the chance to bring them to life.

The power to turn dreams into reality lies in taking active steps. Dreaming is just the beginning; it's committing to action that gives dreams life, leading to incredible achievements that impact our lives and the world.

To make our visions a reality, we need to shift from passive thinking to active doing, dedicating our time, energy, and resources to realising our dreams.

Taking action often involves facing challenges and adapting to unexpected circumstances. With courage and resilience, we can overcome obstacles and realise our dreams.

The philosophy behind "Dream to Action" is centered on the belief that we all have untapped potential, and by cultivating determination and pursuing our dreams, we can ultimately create a life that is not only fulfilling but also meaningful.

Take ownership of your journey towards your goals. Push yourself, for no one else can do it for you. While support helps, the ultimate responsibility lies within you. Embrace your power to make things happen and aim high.

Dreams may require investments, such as time and money, but they provide direction and purpose. Just dreaming without action can lead to unfulfilment. Aligning dreams with action is key to making them a reality.

"Don't let your dreams be dreams." This powerful reminder urges us to act on our aspirations. Achieving dreams requires hard work, perseverance, and overcoming challenges. Set clear goals, break them down into manageable steps, and track your progress.

A network of supportive individuals can be a driving force behind one's motivation and success. If you're determined to achieve your dreams, then it's crucial that you invest time and effort in practical steps, such as acquiring new skills and staying committed to your chosen path.

Overcome fear and doubt to pursue your dreams actively. This journey leads to personal growth, fulfillment, and a purpose-driven life.

Each morning, we face a choice–passively holding onto dreams or actively chasing them. Waking up and pursuing dreams opens us up to possibilities, shaping our lives and creating the future we desire. Don't waste time on idle dreaming; use each day to make progress and move closer to your aspirations.

So, when faced with the choice, find the motivation to wake up, embrace the day, and actively chase your dreams. Make your dreams a remarkable part of your reality, embracing the power of action. Dream big, take action, and enjoy the fulfilling journey to realising your aspirations.

31ST DECEMBER

A DATE CLOSE TO MY HEART

"Working hard and working smart sometimes can be two different things."

– Byron Dorgan

As I contemplate my journey in event management, celebrations and accomplishments, one moment specifically comes to mind - the time when I opted to modernise New Year's Eve events for hotels. With the confidence gained from my past successful events, I knew it was time to take a leap forward. My determination to bring my vision to life led me to increase our team size and implement greater organization and professionalism in New Year's Eve events.

With determination, I crafted unique plans and themes and eagerly presented them to various hotels. Fortunately, they loved the ideas, and word spread about our innovative concept. We offered attractive packages that not only benefited the hotels but also ensured the success of their events. I held a strong conviction that through the delivery of captivating entertainment proposals and exceptional productions, we could establish a lasting impression on our guests, encouraging their recurrent patronage while bolstering the reputation of both the venue and the event.

The memories of our first new year's eve collaborating with five hotels are engraved vividly in my mind. Over time, our reach expanded, and we had the privilege of managing over 30 venues in a single night for many years. Our influence spread across the entire UAE, from Dubai to Ras Al Khaimah, Fujairah to Al Aqah, Alain to Abu Dhabi, and even extending our endeavours to Oman.

The opportunity to work with such varied venues has enabled me to gain priceless experience, broaden my professional connections, and cement our standing as a dependable and sought-after event management enterprise. The New Year's Eve events have become highly expected highlights on our annual calendar, and I am proud to have contributed to the success of many celebrations throughout the region.

To make these events truly spectacular, we left no stone unturned. We selected over 55 talented entertainers and bands, some sourced from Europe while others were local to the UAE. Our team of dedicated staff members ensures a mind-blowing sound experience through the utilisation of state-of-the-art equipment. We set up an impeccable assortment of sound systems, lighting, stages, backdrops, lasers, digital countdowns, and synchronised fireworks. As the clock struck midnight on New Year's Eve, my phone would receive an abundance of calls from appreciative hoteliers expressing their profound appreciation for the faultless execution of their event.

Preparing for this grand day required months of intensive work. Starting in July, I delved into painstaking planning, organising every detail to ensure everything was in place by November. Those five months were undoubtedly stressful, but the joy and gratitude expressed by the hotels made it all worthwhile.

For me, December 31st is not just an ordinary day. It symbolises the peak of a year's worth of hard work, planning, and dedication. It represents the peak of celebration and excitement as people bid farewell to the old year and welcome the new one.

Throughout my event management career, December 31st has always held significant importance. Managing multiple events on this day has been a monumental task, with the demand for exceptional New Year's Eve experiences reaching its peak.

I distinctly recall the excitement that filled the air as the clock drew closer to midnight. The dynamic energy fuelled my drive to guarantee the successful outcome of every event I managed. My team and I worked tirelessly from early morning to late night to ensure flawless celebrations at various venues across the UAE and beyond. The pressure was substantial; however, the rewards were equally significant.

When the clock finally struck midnight on New Year's Day, and the festivities were in full swing, a sense of satisfaction washed over me. I came to the realisation during this journey that the management of large event setups in different locations required a distinct approach. It required forward planning, imaginative brainstorming, methodical orchestration, a devoted team, and an unrelenting quest for success.

DECEMBER 31ST: THE SYMBOLIC DATE OF RESILIENCE, PASSION, AND ACHIEVEMENT

The importance of December 31st is not limited to reflecting on the achievements of the past year. Additionally, it represents our perseverance and determination in overcoming challenges and realising our aspirations. The symbol signifies overcoming obstacles and persevering through hardships, emphasising our resilience and persistence that pushed us forward. The date symbolises our capacity to navigate through difficult times, adjust to evolving circumstances, and emerge more robust than ever. It reminds us of the power of resilience and the capacity to turn obstacles into stepping stones towards success. December 31st is a reminder of our ability to rise above adversity, reclaim our dreams, and forge a path towards a brighter future.

To quote Matthew McConaughey, "Man who invented the hamburger was smart; man who invented the cheeseburger was a genius".

PATH TO SUCCESS

EVENT MANAGEMENT & DAILY LIFE

"Success is not a destination; it's a journey of continous growth and learning."

– Brian Tracy

let's discuss the essential elements vital for succeeding in event management. The ability to master client relationships, refine planning and organisational skills, and effectively manage projects empowers one to navigate industry intricacies proficiently and deliver exceptional events that leave a lasting impression. Prepare yourself to embark on a journey of transformation towards achieving excellence in event management.

BELIEVE IN YOURSELF

Believing in yourself is indeed a crucial step towards achieving success. When you have self-belief, you develop a strong sense of confidence, which are essential qualities for pursuing your goals and dreams.

It is important to remember that no one can dream or believe in your abilities more than you can. Although the support and encouragement of others are valuable, genuine success originates from self-confidence. Have faith in yourself, acknowledge your strengths, improve your weaknesses, and trust in your ability to accomplish extraordinary feats.

PERSONAL TAGLINE FOR SUCCESS IN LIFE

Having a tagline for your success in life is not just for organisations; it's equally valuable for individuals. It serves as a guiding principle, reminding you of your aspirations and motivating you to take action towards achieving your goals. Your personal tagline can be a powerful tool to help you stay focused, inspired, and driven on your journey to success.

"Dream to action!" is my personal tagline, for instance. It's a reminder that dreaming is free and with no limitations, and I can bring them to life by putting them into action.

Your personal tagline can evolve as you achieve milestones, and your priorities shift. It's a reflection of your current mindset and acts as a compass to keep you on track. You can update and refine your tagline as you progress on your journey and gain new insights about yourself and what you want to accomplish.

Similar to how a tagline adds value to a company's brand, a personal tagline adds value to your life. It serves as a constant reminder of your purpose, values, and the direction you want to take. It helps you align your thoughts, beliefs, and actions with your aspirations, guiding you towards success.

To create your personal tagline, start by reflecting on your dreams, passions, and values. Consider what truly motivates and excites you, as well as the impact you want to make in your life and the lives of others. Your tagline should vibrate with you on a deep level, capturing the essence of who you are and what you aspire to achieve.

It's not just about what you think; it's about how you act. Your personal tagline should inspire you to take consistent and purposeful action towards your goals. It should serve as a constant reminder to stay committed, resilient, and focused on your journey to success.

By embracing a personal tagline, you can infuse your daily life with purpose, clarity, and motivation. It becomes a powerful tool that drives you to push beyond limitations, overcome obstacles, and turn your dreams into reality. So, take the time to define your personal tagline and let it guide you towards a life of fulfilment, accomplishment, and success.

OPPORTUNITIES DON'T HAPPEN, YOU NEED TO CREATE THEM

You can't just wait for good things to come your way. Instead, you have the power to make things happen for yourself.

Opportunities can be likened to doors that lead to success or new experiences. Instead of relying on the manifestation of doors, you are empowered to create them yourself. The subject pertains to seizing command of your life and actively pursuing opportunities to advance and reach your objectives.

Creating opportunities requires being proactive and taking action. It means being aware of what you want to achieve and actively working towards it. You might need to network with people, learn new skills, or explore different paths. By taking the initiative, you can open up new possibilities that may not have existed otherwise.

Sometimes, we might think that opportunities are rare or that luck plays the biggest role in success. However, this mindset holds us back. When we believe we can create opportunities, we shift our focus from waiting for the right moment to actively pursuing our goals. It's about embracing the idea that you have the power to shape your own destiny.

Think of it as being the captain of your own ship. You navigate the waters and steer towards the destinations you want to reach. It might involve taking risks, facing challenges, and being tough. But by creating your own opportunities, you increase your chances of success and personal growth.

So, remember, don't wait for opportunities to come knocking on your door. Instead, take the initiative, be proactive, and create your own doors of opportunity. With determination and action, you can shape a future that aligns with your dreams and aspirations.

Push yourself because no one else will do it for you

To succeed, you must motivate and challenge yourself. Others can support you, but it's up to you to make your dreams a reality.

Be your own cheerleader and keep pushing yourself, even in tough times. Take responsibility for your actions and outcomes. Your efforts determine your results.

While others may support you, take control of your own journey and make decisions that align with your dreams.

Your dreams are in your hands. Embrace self-motivation, accountability, personal growth, and independence to turn your dreams into reality.

TIMELY EXECUTION GAINS TRUST AND BENEFITS

Maintaining time is a crucial factor in event management, as clients rely on event managers to ensure that their events run smoothly and on schedule. Effective time management becomes paramount for corporate clients and star hotels and resorts, given their stringent schedules and deadlines.

By delivering events promptly and according to schedule, you exhibit your professionalism and dependability, fostering a reputation for providing superior services. As a result of this, clients may provide repeat business and referrals, as they have confidence in your ability to execute successful events consistently.

The timely delivery of events is a crucial element of event management, and by ensuring that events are delivered promptly and with excellence, you can establish a strong reputation and attract prestigious clients.

CREATIVE - COMMITTED - CANDID

Yes, being committed, creative, and candid are important qualities for success in any field, including event management. Here's why:

Commitment: Event management can be a demanding and challenging field, requiring long hours, hard work, and a willingness to go above and beyond to ensure that events are successful. By being committed to your work, you show to clients and colleagues that you are dedicated to delivering the best possible results.

Creative: The ability to be creative is crucial in event management as it allows for differentiation from competitors and the provision of exceptional experiences to both clients and attendees. By coming up with innovative and unique concepts, you can create events that capture the imagination and leave a lasting impression.

Candid: The crucial role of honesty and transparency in event management stems from the clients' reliance on accurate information, advice, and feedback from event managers. Straightforward communication can foster positive relationships based on mutual respect and understanding, building trust with clients.

In the fast-paced business world, many believe that working late and sacrificing family time is necessary for success. However, I want to challenge this notion and offer a different perspective. You don't have to compromise your family for lasting success.

True success goes beyond the number of hours you spend working. It involves finding a balance that allows you to excel in your career while also nurturing other vital aspects of your life, such as your family, personal well-being, and leisure time.

Personally, I had made a deliberate decision to give priority to my family, especially to ensure that my daughters were well-cared for and well-prepared for each day. My success was not hindered by this choice.

Achieving success without sacrificing time with your loved ones requires efficiency and effectiveness. By focusing on essential tasks, setting clear goals, and prioritising what truly matters, you can attain your objectives while still dedicating quality time to your family.

Taking care of yourself and your family actually enhances your professional performance. Striking a work-life balance reduces stress, enhances mental and physical well-being, and stimulates creativity, focus, and productivity. When you prioritise self-care and family time, you become better equipped to excel in your job and achieve even greater success.

It's crucial to understand that success does not involve choosing between work and family. Rather, it's about integrating and harmonising both aspects of your life. By giving priority to what truly matters and managing your time mindfully, you can attain enduring success while simultaneously enjoying a fulfilling personal life.

Maintaining a balance between work and family is an ongoing challenge; however, it is imperative to prioritise family time, even during busy work periods. Creating a healthy balance and enduring memories with your loved ones causes the establishment of boundaries, planning of meaningful activities, delegation of tasks, and prudent use of technology.

It is imperative to remember success encompasses not only professional accomplishments but also the love, connection, and happiness shared within your family.

MY TOOLBOX

FOR EVENT MANAGEMENT SUCCESS

"Your work is going to fill a large part of your life, and the only way to be truly satisfied is to do what you believe is great work. And the only way to do great work is to love what you do."

– Steve Jobs.

When I started on my journey in event planning, the concept was relatively unknown. Back in the late 90s, the idea of event planning had gained little recognition. I observed the busy schedules of hoteliers, especially those in the food and beverage industry, and it sparked an idea. I thought to myself: why not offer my services to help them and simultaneously make a living from it?

The hoteliers would individually reach out to suppliers when hosting an event. This process consumed a significant amount of their time and effort. That's when I came up to be "a one-stop event and entertainment solutions partner". By being a single point of contact, I could handle all their event planning needs. I took on the responsibility of managing payments to suppliers and entertainers, making the job much easier for everyone involved.

My aim was to simplify the event planning process and ease the burden from the hoteliers. They could rely on me to coordinate and manage all the arrangements, allowing them to focus on their core responsibilities. This approach not only saved them time but also provided convenience and peace of mind.

I found great satisfaction in event planning. Witnessing the successful execution of events was deeply fulfilling, knowing that I played a pivotal role in making them happen.

EVENT MANAGEMENT- A SERIOUS BUSINESS

Event management is indeed a serious business. When organising an event, there's no room for mistakes or second chances. Once the event starts, it's a live experience, and any problems or errors can affect its success. Consider a wedding, for example. Imagine if I forget to inform the emcee about the exact time to start the event. The guests have arrived on time, eagerly waiting for the festivities to begin. However, because of the delay caused by the emcee's late start, the event loses its momentum, and the overall experience is compromised. The true essence of an event is found in its spontaneous moments.

The same holds true for other events like product launches, anniversaries, or birthdays. Each event has its own goals, and mistakes can have lasting effects. As an event manager, take event management seriously and always work with dedication and professionalism.

My goal was always to exceed expectations and provide clients with a successful event that leaves an unforgettable mark. It needs precise planning and skilled execution. By recognising the importance of getting it right the first time, I ensured that my client's events were successful, memorable, and left no room for regret.

WHAT MAIN QUALITIES SHOULD AN EVENT PLANNER HAVE?

An event planner should possess qualities such as dedication, commitment, and punctuality. It is essential for them to be punctual and arrive on time for the event planning process. Being punctual allows the planner to focus on the details and effectively manage the event, avoiding unnecessary rush or chaos. By showing up on time, the planner can approach their work with a sense of calmness to ensure that nothing important is missed.

QUALIFICATIONS REQUIRED FOR AN EVENT PLANNER

While there aren't any specific educational requirements, communication skills, which can be developed on the job, are essential for career progression. Although now days, higher qualifications often open up better opportunities in the field as there are many existing event related courses.

Event planning is a highly sought-after profession because of the booming industry and the need for event planners in various sectors. FMCG companies may require help to introduce their products. Popular events include product launches, weddings, birthdays, and anniversaries.

IS EVENT PLANNING A STRESSFUL JOB?

Event planning is undoubtedly a high-pressure job. From start to finish, the pressure is always on. Late nights, early mornings, and limited sleep can cause stress. You may encounter difficult clients to deal with.

There are several disadvantages to being an event planner. Job instability, unusual work hours, and separation from family and friends are all part of the job. However, as the saying goes, "no pain, no gain". While the initial stages may be challenging, once you overcome them, you can reap the benefits of being an event planner. You can earn more, become highly sought after, and the market will pay you what you ask for. This is when you realise that smart work pays off.

PRICE IS WHAT YOU PAY, VALUE IS WHAT YOU GET

The phrase "price is what you pay, value is what you get" means that the actual worth of your service is not solely based on price. Price isn't everything. Consider the quality, benefits, usefulness, or satisfaction you experience when you use the product. Expensive items may provide more value than cheaper options.

For example, let's say you need to rent a sound system for an event. You get two quotes from different companies, and one is more expensive because it has better sound quality and technical capabilities. Paying more for better sound quality is justifiable.

'Price is what you pay, value is what you get' is a reminder to prioritise the value we'll receive over the cost of a purchase. This principle holds particular significance while planning special events like weddings. Unlike products that can be refunded or exchanged, events are singular and cannot be easily altered once the day arrives. A budget-friendly wedding package may seem attractive, but there are no adjustments or refunds if it doesn't meet expectations. It is crucial to assess thoroughly the value you are receiving in relation to the price you are paying. Research the service provider's reputation and reviews.

Make more informed decisions by understanding the importance of value for money. This way, you can avoid disappointment and ensure that your special event is truly memorable and enjoyable.

To round things up, here are a couple of pointers to keep in mind when planning your event:

VALUE OVER PRICE

Consider the value you will receive in terms of quality, services and overall experience. A slightly higher price might be worth it if it ensures a smoother and more memorable event.

CHOOSE REPUTABLE SERVICE PROVIDERS

Read reviews, check their track record, and ask for recommendations. Trusted professionals will ensure a successful event.

DELEGATE AND COLLABORATE

Avoid the temptation to handle everything on your own. Build a team of competent individuals and delegate responsibilities accordingly. Collaboration allows for diverse perspectives and ensures that tasks are managed efficiently. Remember, teamwork makes the dream work!

Visit event venues in person to assess suitability

Consider transportation, timing, and setup to avoid last-minute issues.

COMMUNICATE CLEARLY AND CONSISTENTLY

Effective communication is key to event success. Maintain open lines of communication with all involved parties, including suppliers, vendors, and clients. Clearly convey expectations, timelines, and any changes or updates. Regular communication ensures everyone is on the same page and reduces the likelihood of misunderstandings.

BE PREPARED FOR THE UNEXPECTED

Stay calm, think on your feet, and be prepared with backup plans or alternative solutions. Adaptability and flexibility are essential qualities for event planners to handle unforeseen challenges.

TAKE CARE OF YOURSELF

Event planning can be demanding and stressful. Remember to prioritise self-care and maintain a healthy work-life balance. Take breaks, delegate when necessary, and seek support from your team or network. Your well-being directly impacts your ability to deliver successful events.

Follow these guidelines to make your event memorable and successful. Event management involves dedication, professionalism and creating unforgettable experiences.

MY PASSION – MY LIFE

EMBRACING THE WAY OF LIFE

"The journey of a thousand miles begins with a single step."

– Lao Tzu

Throughout a career spanning over 20 years, I have had the privilege of orchestrating and executing many successful events, leaving an indelible mark on the field of event coordination and entertainment. Pursuing my childhood passion for karate led me to discover a sense of fulfilment that impacted both my personal and professional life.

I am grateful for the opportunities that allowed me to pursue work I truly enjoyed. I made a conscious decision to prioritise joy and satisfaction, and this approach kept me motivated every step of the way.

However, there came a point when I realised the need for change. I understood that true fulfilment comes from aligning with our deepest desires and embracing a healthier, more balanced lifestyle. This realisation prompted me to step back from the events business and embark on a new chapter.

When I was a kid in the 80s, I was fascinated by karate movies that were popular in India. So, my friend and I decided to search for a karate school on our own. Every day, we went for long walks, hoping to find any signs of a dojo. We looked everywhere but couldn't find one. It was disappointing, and we had no choice but to focus on other things like school and hobbies, putting our love for martial arts on hold.

As time went by, my friend and I followed different paths in our careers and ended up in different countries. We had to face the challenges and demands of life, and unfortunately, karate had to take a backseat during that period. Our passion for karate had to be temporarily set aside as we prioritised our responsibilities and adapted to new environments. It was a sacrifice that was deemed necessary at that time.

However, despite putting karate aside, the desire to practise it never completely faded away. It remained a dear memory and a dream I hoped to revisit someday. While waiting for my child's school bus, I came across an advertisement on a passing karate school bus after several years of being occupied with my business and family. It seized my attention and reminded me of my past attraction to karate. The incident stimulated a feeling of excitement and prompted me to reconsider my interest in pursuing karate. It felt like a sign, motivating me to take action and prioritise my own personal growth. That advertisement became a symbol of hope, reigniting my passion for karate and inspiring me to pursue it once more.

Considering the advertisement and my renewed passion for karate, I promptly enrolled my daughters in the karate school. Watching their progress and involvement in the courses helped me understand the importance of pursuing my own goals. Despite my hectic schedule, I made the brave decision to join myself.

I recognised that juggling my responsibilities would be challenging, but I was determined to make it work. I didn't want to let this opportunity pass me by. So, side by side with my daughters, I began my journey of training in karate.

Joining the karate class was a significant step for me. It meant prioritising my personal fulfilment amidst my busy life. It was a decision that showed I was dedicated to improving myself and pursuing what truly mattered to me.

Despite the hurdles of managing my time and energy, I embraced the challenges wholeheartedly. Training in karate brought back the joy and satisfaction I had longed for, and it allowed me to reconnect with a part of myself that I had set aside for far too long.

This experience has granted me the understanding that despite the direction life takes us on or the difficulties it presents, our dreams and passions can resurface without warning. It's always possible to reconnect with our interests and pursue what truly brings us happiness.

To stay motivated and committed to karate, I found a training partner. Having someone to train with made it harder for me to skip classes and do other fun activities instead. I felt responsible and didn't want to miss out on pursuing my favourite hobby.

As time passed, I prepared for my black belt test, a significant achievement in the world of karate. I revived my childhood passion and established a martial arts academy to inspire and empowering people. My decision has revitalised my sense of purpose and granted me a deep sense of contentment. Every day at the academy brings me great joy as I impart my knowledge.

As much as managing time is significant in events, it is also just as significant for my dojo. I make it clear to my students that karate is all about discipline, and the first discipline is to show up on time for class. I believe that instilling this value from a young age will benefit them in the long run, and I am confident that time will reward them.

A childhood dream of advocating for karate and physical well-being came to mind during this experience. The idea of starting my dojo and sharing my knowledge with others brought me immense joy. My primary goal was to see my students apply the principles they learned from karate and reaping its benefits in their daily lives.

I wanted to create a space where people could learn and practice karate, especially in an area where it wasn't readily accessible. The memories of my childhood days spent searching for a dojo to train in resonated strongly within me.

I saw a place where individuals of all ages and backgrounds could come together, united by their shared passion for karate. My dojo would not only be a space for physical training but also a hub for personal growth, discipline, and self-improvement. I wanted to create an environment that promoted respect, dedication, and a strong sense of community.

Karate is not just about physical moves and techniques. It also strengthens the mind and body. It improves coordination, stamina, reflexes, and overall health. Karate teaches important values, like discipline, focus, and confidence. I always encourage parents and children to explore the world of martial arts and experience the positive effects it can have on their lives.

Karate has become an integral part of my life and it has transcended beyond being just a hobby for me. It's a way of life. This thing has become a part of me and I cannot imagine my life without it. Thanks to my involvement with the dojo, I have been granted the opportunity to inspire and help others in their journey to improve their overall well-being, both physically and mentally.

It is essential to note that, in karate, the importance of repetition and concentration is underscored by this method. The consistent repetition of a singular action can improve one's abilities, cultivate cognitive strength, and promote unwavering concentration.

It is never too late to embark on a journey of learning or engage in activities that promote physical fitness, such as karate or any other form of exercise. Age should never be seen as a barrier to personal growth, development, or pursuing new interests.

Taking up karate or any form of fitness at any stage of life can be a transformative experience. It offers many benefits, including improved physical strength, flexibility, balance, and cardiovascular health.

The journey of personal growth and fitness is unique to each individual, and progress is measured by your personal improvement rather than comparisons to others.

A JOURNEY OF PASSION AND PURPOSE

Life is too precious to spend on joyless work. Embrace your passions, prioritise balance and health, and find fulfilment in all you do. Create a life where work feels like a labour of love, filled with purpose and contentment.

I selectively collaborate with like-minded professionals who share my work style. This approach brings me immense satisfaction as I witness the happiness of my clients and partners.

Take a moment to reflect on your own life and the choices you've made. Embrace joy and fulfilment, for they are the keys to personal happiness and success. When we align our passions with our pursuits, we not only thrive, but also leave a lasting impact on the world.

Faced with challenges and uncertainty, my journey as a business owner is proof of the power of belief and determination. With unwavering faith in myself and my vision, I overcame obstacles, learned, and grew. Through hard work, resilience, and a passion for making a difference, I created a successful and impactful business. Achieving remarkable things is possible with the right mindset and a positive outlook.

Thank you for accompanying me on this journey. I hope this book will help guide you on your path to success.

TESTIMONIALS

JANE SALOS CHA, CWC, CFO BUSINESS MANAGER

Rocky and his team were instrumental in booking Paul Salos, The Voice of Sinatra and The Let's Dance Band for a very special and elegant wedding at the exclusive Madinat Jumeirah Arabian Resort-Dubai, a luxurious 5 Star Resort. The Madinat Jumeirah is the largest resort in the Emirate. It was a spectacular wedding with over 950 guests. Paul Salas, the female vocalist and the Let's Dance Band were a huge success.

Rocky and his team went out of their way to ascertain that Paul Salos, the female vocalist and the Band were taken care of during their travels from the United States, accommodations, meals and all necessities while in Dubai.

Rocky and his team also did an excellent job with the setup, sound equipment, rehearsal, and lighting for Paul Salos and the band members. We appreciate Rocky and his team for the management and follow through with a flawless and excellent event. Paul Salos and The Let's Dance Band would be available for any booking that Rocky and his team would have for them and would not hesitate in recommending Rocky & his team for any event.

Thank you,

SIDNEY KILONGA - BAND LEADER, MOMBASA KENYA EAST AFRICA

As I arrived in the U.A.E., the year late 2003,... I really hustled a lot to get a good contract, but in vain. Luck came to me as i came across my dream come true promotion & events management company. Rocky and your wonderful team came to my rescue. I remember this year very well. It was early 2004.

Here we came into a contract and well signed, never to regret up to now. What a blessing it was to me and my good family. I remember very well being given good shows and hotel contracts never to forget around the U.A.E by you., Those were the days,..we used to be playing in Fujairah, Ras Al Khaimah, Abu Dhabi hotels,.. just to mention but a few. Dubai was my home with various hotels enjoying our entertainments with lovely shows. I remember the Dubai shopping festivals,.. the festive Christmas, New Year parties,. Eid .Money,.. money,.. money,..hahaha, just name it.

Truly, we enjoyed the company of your faithful team who was always there for us. The relationship was well taken care of,.. thank you so much Mr. Rocky. From Rocky & Team,.. I managed to achieve my goals. I bought a piece of land in my good country and constructed my beautiful house of which up to now my children are enjoying the fruits of my benefits. Ooh, last but not least,.. my great wish is to continue working with you once more and enjoy the love of a great faithful ROCKY & TEAM.

OLSON FERNANDES

CONSULTANT AT KREUZ SUBSEA PTE. LTD.

I have known Roque over the years. He is very passionate about his work and loves what he does, ie, the entertainment business. I have seen him grow as a very honest businessman, easy to deal with, plenty of new ideas, and ensures customer satisfaction.

EPIGRAPH

BE CREATIVE: Set your imagination free and allow your creativity to flow without limits.

BE COMMITTED: Put all your heart and soul into your goals and dreams.

BE CANDID: Stay true to who you are. Speak your mind open.

ACTION YOUR DREAMS: Dreams become reality through action.

THINK POSITIVE - WORK SMART - LOVE WHAT YOU DO

ABOUT THE AUTHOR

Everything starts with a dream. It does not cost to dream. Roque Quadros, also known as Rocky, is a visionary entrepreneur, founder, director and martial artist with a strong connection to Goa, India. He grew up in Bombay (Now Mumbai) and from a young age; he believed in the power of actions to shape destinies. For Rocky, knowledge was not enough; it had to be applied in practice to achieve personal growth and development. He has always been passionate about learning, and he embraced everything with enthusiasm and dedication.

Throughout his life, Rocky has been driven by the pursuit of happiness and fulfilment. He never settled for anything that didn't bring him pure joy and sought opportunities aligned with his passions and interests. His journey has taken him from being an air conditioning technician to creating his own travel agency, and later exploring the field of event management and entertainment, where he became a pioneer in providing event management solutions. He managed thousands of international events and built an extensive network of bands and artists in the entertainment industry.

A significant turning point in Rocky's life came when he reflected on his goals and priorities. He made a conscious decision to prioritise his well-being and health over accumulating wealth. This decision is one he takes great pride in, as he believes that good health is the true wealth that forms the foundation for a fulfilling life.

After moving back to India, Rocky pursued his dream of opening a martial arts academy and discovered his passion for teaching martial arts. He is focused on planning and establishing a medical tourism venture in Goa to help patients plan their treatments.

Throughout his journey, Rocky has been a strong advocate for embracing passions, dreaming big, and taking action. He believes that imagination and big dreams are powerful tools for achieving greatness, but they must be backed by action to turn them into reality. His tagline "Think of an event, we make it happen." reflects his commitment to turning dreams into reality. Rocky is an inspiration to others, encouraging them to pursue their passions, find joy in their pursuits, and experience success and personal fulfilment along the way.

ELEVATE YOUR BOOK

PURCHASE WITH A PERSONALIZED CONSULTATION

As the author of this empowering book, I'm thrilled to introduce a value-added incentive that goes beyond the pages. When you purchase my book, you're not just gaining valuable insights—you're also unlocking a door to a one-on-one conversation with me, where we can dive deeper into your aspirations and goals. Here's how this exciting opportunity works:

1. THE OFFER EXPLAINED:

Immerse yourself in the knowledge contained within my book, and as a token of appreciation, receive a complimentary 15-minute personalized consultation session. Whether you're considering venturing into the event management industry or seeking guidance on pursuing a thriving career in events, this exclusive offer is tailored to empower your journey.

2. WHAT TO EXPECT:

During our insightful 15-minute conversation, we'll delve into the topics most relevant to you. Whether you're eager to launch your own event management venture or eager to gain a foothold in this vibrant industry, I'm here to provide guidance, advice, and a roadmap tailored to your aspirations.

3. SPREADING THE WORD:

Join me on this journey by spreading the word about this unique offer.

4. THE VALUE YOU'LL GAIN:

Imagine the insights you'll gather from our focused conversation—expertise distilled from my years in the events industry. This personalized session is a chance to gain a competitive edge, a strategic plan, or even a burst of inspiration, all customized to your journey.

5. TAILORED JUST FOR YOU:

This isn't a one-size-fits-all interaction. I'm committed to personalizing our talk to align with your dreams and goals. Your success story matters, and this conversation is designed to propel you toward it.

This unique opportunity is more than a token—it's a chance to connect, to learn, and to grow. By taking your book experience a step further, you're investing in a personalized journey toward success in the events industry. Together, we'll unlock doors and create pathways to achievement.

www.ingramcontent.com/pod-product-compliance
Lightning Source LLC
LaVergne TN
LVHW091048150826
845673LV00002B/506

* 9 7 9 8 8 9 0 6 6 8 6 5 3 *